Praise for

Living **DOUBLE**

"*Living Double* is an excellent account of the power of perseverance, and also the power of love -- not just the love JaNeika and JaSheika have for the art of writing television, but also the love and support the sisters have for each other. As someone who often works with her sister, I am impressed by the story of these two women's shared dream and their journey to bring it to fruition. This book will inspire anyone to follow their dreams."

—**Attica Locke,** Writer/Producer of *Little Fires Everywhere, When They See Us*, Edgar Award-Winning Author of *Bluebird, Bluebird and Heaven, My Home*

"Reading this book feels like having a "come to Jesus" discussion with your Sistah Girl group, when you need it the most. This is the Group Chat of encouragement, needed at the beginning, the middle and the end of your journey into your dreams. A wonderfully poignant peak into how many years, overnight success, really takes. How fear and doubt are both important ingredients for bravery and tenacity. JaNeika and JaSheika are the perfect duality of identical opposites. In their story of growth, strength, and the importance of television to latchkey kids, *Living Double* is the exact cheering section you want, sitting on your shoulders as you walk through to the scariest and most fulfilling triumphs of your life. Much like interning, wishing isn't for the faint of heart."

—**Gabourey Sidibe,** Oscar-Nominated Actress and Author of *This Is Just My Face*

"Ranging from heartfelt stories of their upbringing to deeply personal insight of life lessons learned, JaNeika and JaSheika James achieve the goal of crafting a slice of life that everyone can relate to. More than a triumph of industry, Hollywood or otherwise, this book illustrates the triumph of one's soul. A terrific read; an even more inspiring narrative!"

—**Trai & Grace Byers**, NAACP-Nominated Actor, Actress and New York Times Best-Selling Author of *I Am Enough* and *I Believe I Can*

"This Hollywood game can be exhausting. From racial and gender inequality, ulterior motives, and all the other foolishness that goes along with it. When you come into contact with two beautiful humans like JaNeika and JaSheika, somehow the world gets brighter. Writers and Executive Producers who are amazing at their jobs, but equally incredible, loyal and righteous human beings. I'm so happy their story is being told with such humor and heart. *Living Double* is not only a guide to chasing your dreams but it's also a testament to the strength, endurance and love that lays deep in the fabric of who these two Queens are."

—**Jussie Smollett**, Emmy-Nominated Producer, Director, Actor, Singer, Songwriter

"Stick together. Ignore the haters. Find your tribe." – Just a sample of the pearls Jasheika and Janeika share in this must-read for all the soap-obsessed kids out there who grew up fighting with their mothers over weekday VCR abuses. *Living Double* is a reminder that our journeys in this business are as unique as the dreams that set us on those paths in the first place. Just one nagging question: Which one of you is the evil twin??!"

—**Mike Kelley**, Creator and Executive Producer of *Revenge*

"The James Twin's extraordinary tale strikes a match for people longing to ignite their wildest dreams. JaNeika and JaSheika blaze over outdated barriers with courage, grit, and determination times two. I adore how this book celebrates sisterly love, reminding me that life's real power comes from the unconditional bonds we cultivate with family, friends, and creative partnerships."

—**Wendy Calhoun**, Writer/Producer of *Empire*, *Revenge*, *Nashville*, and *Justified*

"As a twin sister myself, reading JaNeika and JaSheika's story from sisterly love to success is one I relate to and admire. From their practical advice–straight with no chaser–to their inspirational journey of faith and triumph in Hollywood, *Living Double* is an entertaining and insightful guide for sisters, women, and anyone daring to dream big with exceeding and abundant faith."

—**Tasha Smith**, Actress, Director, Producer, and Founder of the Tasha Smith Actors Workshop

"This walk down memory lane is so much more than your average "How to Do Hollywood" book. The James' twins share their journey with such honesty and vulnerability. It's a big ole plate of hope and empowerment seasoned with all kinds of "black girl magic" and should be read by anyone who is trying to follow their dreams in Hollywood. It is a love letter to hustle and a great example of how each brick, each victory, each failure builds the track that keeps the training moving forward."

— **Karin Gist**, Executive Producer/Showrunner/Writer, *Star*, *Mixed-ish*, *Grey's Anatomy*, *Revenge*

"*Living Double* is a beautiful guide to success because it's all about believing in yourself. JaNeika and JaSheika share their unique journey in a way that's universally relatable, practical and also fun to read. If you're not lucky enough to be able to chat with them over a cocktail, this book is the next best thing."

—**Jennifer Crittenden**, Emmy-Winning Executive Producer of *Housebroken*; *Veep*, *New Adventures of Old Christine*, *Everybody Loves Raymond*, *Seinfeld*

"As someone who's been in the TV business since the late nineties, I was surprised at how inspired I was after reading *Living Double*. JaNeika and JaSheika are hard-working, dedicated and extremely talented, following their journey to success and creative fulfillment totally reignited me and reminded me why I love what I do. Whether you are just starting out, or have been in this business for years, this book has so much to offer about how to approach your dreams."

—**Gabrielle Allan**, Emmy-Winning Executive Producer of *Housebroken*; *Veep*, *Divorce*, *Scrubs*

"I wish *Living Double* was around when I was trying to break into the industry. The James Sisters have somehow managed to take years of experience on some of TV's most successful shows and distill it into an extremely insightful, accurate -- and damn entertaining -- guide to writing and producing television. If you've ever dreamed of writing for TV, this book is a MUST."

—**Joe Fazzio**, Writer and Co-Executive Producer of *Revenge* and *How to Get Away with Murder*

"Whether or not you grew up idolizing *All My Children*'s Erica Kane and *Living Single*'s Khadijah, you will be inspired by the journey of JaNeika and JaSheika James. Like television's most compelling heroines, they are smart, soulful, and driven women who refused to limit their dreams and charted a path to success. Their book will make you smile, think, and help you take a step towards your own beautiful future."

—**Maggie Malina**, Executive Producer of *Hit the Floor* and *CrazySexyCool: The TLC Story*

Living DOUBLE

HOW IDENTICAL TWINS UNLOCKED THE DOOR TO SUCCESS IN HOLLYWOOD

JANEIKA JAMES & JASHEIKA JAMES

Editorial Project Management: Karen Rowe, karen@karenrowe.com
Cover Design: Beatrice Sims
Cover Design and Photograph: Walid Azami
Inside Layout: Deana Riddle

Printed in the United States of America
FIRST EDITION

ISBN: 978-1-7358968-0-9 (print)
ISBN: 978-1-7358968-1-6 (.mobi)
ISBN: 978-1-7358968-2-3 (.epub)

Published by
PWR Press
1205 N. Franklin St. Suite 214
Tampa, FL, 33602
www.pwrpresspublishing.com

For Ma and Granddaddy Cliff:

Thank you for planting our spirits with the seeds of dreams
— In this lifetime and beyond.

Contents

Living **DOUBLE**

Foreword by Yvette Lee Bowser

"No matter how little people may expect you to accomplish as a Black girl, the universe has big plans for you. You will exceed those plans."

— Yvette Lee (1977)

I was twelve when I wrote this in my diary—which my mother read often to know what I was up to. She was so nosey and concerned. But with good cause. The world was filled with negative imagery and messages for anyone who looked like me (a "confused-haired" Black girl). So much so that I'd taken to writing daily affirmations long before they were trendy.

I felt invisible... but I was determined not to be. I always dreamt of telling stories —MY stories, stories that challenged the narrative that Blacks and women were only on this planet to play supporting roles. Fortunately, my first attempt at a series was *"Living Single."* Somehow, I defied the odds, becoming the first Black woman to create a hit TV show... in 1993. Crazy, right? But WHO tells our stories matters. And Black women have always fought the odds and flourished defiantly. JaNeika and JaSheika James continue that tradition in their debut book. Part memoir, part how-to, *Living Double* is a refreshing guide to overcoming the nattering nabobs of negativity who don't want you to be great. This book could easily be titled *Exceeding Expectations in Glorious Fashion*. That is precisely what JaNeika and JaSheika have done in an industry that doesn't always appreciate and amplify all that is magical and beautiful about us.

In being "the first," I've always felt a tremendous responsibility to make sure I wasn't the last. It's been an honor to mentor "The Twins." It's also deeply humbling to know that these beautiful, brilliant young women were, in any small part, encouraged by my journey the way the details of their ascent reinvigorated me. If you're looking for a lift to get over that "I-can't-do-this" hump, or just a delicious read, turn the page and dive in.

Go and be great! You can't help but be inspired to do so after reading *Living Double.*

Yvette Lee Bowser (2020)

Foreword by Mioshi Hill

"If ever there was proof that black girl magic exists, you will find it in the chambers of the heart. It lives in the space that links soul to spirit; slumbering beside fear and muse alike. And when we wake it, its sweet sound breaks the silence of our deepest desires... A crisp cackle, a bell chime... as a dream springs to life."

— Mioshi Hill (2019)

If you were to wander onto the dreamscape of JaNeika and JaSheika James, it would look like the wonderland of a vintage studio lot. Stroll down the white-washed sidewalks of *La La Land* aligned with the razor sharp emerald hedges of *Edward Scissorhands*. Listen well and you'll hear the soft trickle of *Dawson's Creek* in the background—its tranquil melody disrupted with horn blasts of morning traffic as four sistas *Living Single* hustle off to big jobs in a "90s kind of world." Sirens lead you to the gates of *General Hospital;* onlookers and bystanders pressed around the entrance to see who shot Sonny... or perhaps that's J.R. up from *Dallas*? The wind whips through your hair as you look up to the awesome sight of Harry Potter's soaring broom in a game of Quidditch. Yes, this is in fact *A Different World*, as you pass the Hillman college campus, bustling with bright, young people eager to change the world.

Your senses are now on overload. The mouth-watering aroma of grilled burgers and fries waft from 90210's Peach Pit. The resounding crisp smack of Erica Kane slapping a quarreling lover... swift movement to your right as *Buffy the Vampire Slayer* leaps over an open grave giving chase to a vampire foe. You see, smell and hear everything. You have never felt more alive. And at the center of it all is the maestro of this circus hyperreality. His voice booms at every passerby, including the *Pretty Woman* who crosses his intersection... they share a smile and then he looks beyond her to stare directly at you. You blink and all of a sudden he's gone. In his place stands the James sisters. They wear his grin, his swagger and even the bold tone of his voice as they reach welcoming arms out to you and say his famous line, *"Welcome to Hollywood! What's your dream?"* This book is their welcome to the land of dreams, and I have never met tour guides more equipped to help you navigate manifesting your dreams into reality.

The first lesson I learned from the James sisters was that in order to successfully make your dreams come true, you have to first believe in the dream. Put your ego away, because I'm not talking about having confidence in your ability to accomplish a goal set; that is a kind of conviction required, but not the first step in the process. This is not the belief in self. Nor is this the wishful belief of coin-filled well bottoms, or the risk-taking belief of luck games. To successfully dream, you first need the life-bringer belief... and that is the tricky part; breathing life into the dream.

When I met JaNeika James in graduate school, I was immediately taken by how alive her dreams were. She spoke of our favorite characters in books and on the screen as if they were real people, she had very real experiences with. To say the least, she was... eccentric. I was intrigued with this quirky young woman who was, from my point-of-view, innocent in her realization of fantasy worlds. I mistook her method of dreaming for simple observation; cataloguing and collecting her favorites to study the craft or sprout out for playful trivia. I secretly worried for her... gifted she certainly was, but she would need to put some distance between her and these "dreams" so that her work did not run too close to mimicry. Art imitates life, after all. As artists, we need to dare to live the real-life experiences in order to successfully create artworks around them. Write what you know. JaNeika challenged me on this. *Who's to say the watched experience is not just as real? Did you not compare your first kiss to the first one you saw on the screen?* Well, yes... but that's just an extension of the writer's real experience. OK, but now that you've seen it, now that it's a part of your memory, is it any less real to you if it's the kiss you compare all others to?

A beat. And this is when the believing begins... once it lives in your memory, once it's a fiber in the fabric that makes you you, that moment, that character, that story now has life. It's more than a reflection of the real thing now. It's real on its own in every way. JaNeika knew this secret early in her career. It's not a question whether art imitates life or if life imitates art, dreams are made of both. They are not mutually exclusive, and every single one of the characters, television shows or action sequences she loved as a kid became more than mere symbols or examples of her dream gig... she gave them all life, and they became the dream.

Once I met JaSheika, their life-bringing dreamer methodology became even clearer. They personify two sides of the base word "dream." If as a "dreamer" JaNeika represents the noun version of the word giving real life and purpose to every goal she sets, JaSheika is very much the adjective; dreamy and whimsical in every way. Unlike JaNeika, she is not concerned with the who and what of it all... she brings her dreams to life by focusing in on the what and how. What does it look like? How does it feel? Her dreams come true because she day-dreams up the detail of their existence. Together they both answer the why, and manifest with specificity and clarity every dream they dare to believe in.

But there is a rule of threes in creation and just like the divine muse, there is a third side of the word; to dream as a verb. That is what motivated the James Sisters to write this book. That is where you come in. In this love letter to the dreamer, JaNeika and JaSheika James have plotted out the actions, taken step-by-step and day by-day to bring your dreams to life. There are many paths to success, but hopefully some of their shared knowledge and experience can give you a map to make the journey easier. And if you are anything like me—skeptical of how-to's and self-help gurus—go forward knowing that this is not an altruistic endeavor on the James' part. It begins and ends with respect for the creative. Dreams are not meant to be isolative creatures; life begets life and every successful dreamer seeks to inspire others to dream their dreams. Learn more and dare to create so you can populate the James Twins' dreamscape with the stories, loves and lives that keep the world turning.

So with that, I take you back to that timeless studio lot... Blink, and see that our maestro is still there, waiting to welcome you. He gives you a lop-sided grin, stepping back to make space for you to enter. *"Some dreams come true, some don't, but keep on dreamin' — this Hollywood. Always time to dream, so keep on dreamin."*

Mioshi Jade Hill
Vice President Development & Programming, LIFETIME

Living **DOUBLE**

As twin sisters, *Living Double* is something we've done our entire lives. From the wooooomb to the woooooorld— (in our Lil' Jon *"Get Low"* voices, of course)— we've done pretty much everything you could imagine together. Eating our first meals (thanks Mommy for the milk supply), saying our first words, taking our first steps, getting our first perm that killed our natural hair follicles at four-years old (again, thanks Mommy), and even attending college, together at the University of Florida, in pursuit of a profession that would allow us to continue this double living by eventually working together.

While *Living Double* is a testament to our existence up until this point in our lives, it is also a homage to the show that planted the seed of the first dream we ever shared—to become successful Black women in our own rights; unapologetically, unabashedly, and unafraid. *Living Single,* is the TV show that did just that.

It gave voice to strong, educated, opinionated, motivated, beautiful, Black women of all shapes and shades. As young, impressionable viewers, it provided something for us to look forward to watching every Thursday night, while being enlightened, entertained, and often educated on a number of social and cultural issues of the time. It celebrated Black love, and reminded us that the pursuit of success in both our professional lives, as well as our love lives, does not have to be mutually exclusive. Most importantly, it inspired a generation of women to seek excellence, to be emboldened, and to be empowered by our womanhood, our sisterhood, our intelligence, our independence, our entrepreneurship, our whimsy, and our desire for love—the important stuff that dreams are made of.

Today, *Living Double* is not just a testament, it is our way of acknowledging that our dreams can live both beyond and within the realm of our reality. They can walk alongside each other, occupy the same space at the same time, in a sort of dual existence—like twins.

We pray that every reader who comes across these pages finds a sprinkle of inspiration that calls you to action in the relentless pursuit of <u>YOUR DREAMS</u>, much like *Living Single* inspired ours.

Introduction

Hey You!

Yes, we're talking to you! The smart and curious one who picked up this book and started sifting through the pages to see what, outside of the fabulously gorgeous cover, catches your eye. Yes, you—the beautiful one with impeccable taste.

If you picked up this book, you are probably like us—someone who is wildly passionate about colors and attracted to bright, bold, and beautiful books, and curious to find out how much you relate and identify with the pages behind the cover. We know this because that's what gets us. We are supercharged, inspired and moved by visuals-whether it's books, magazines, art, TV, film, nature, etc.— we get it. We get you-because we *are* you. We are creators. We are dreamers.

This book is a love letter to you and all the other dreamers out there. It is for those who have dreams but are either afraid to take the risk, or don't have any idea how or where to begin to make them come true. Writing this book took us on a journey down memory lane, reminding us what it felt like to be in the position you are in right now.

To be honest, we had a lot of initial trepidation with the idea of writing this book. We didn't really want to "go there"—mainly because we are BTSS: Behind the Scenes Sistas! We intentionally work behind the scenes because being on the other side isn't necessarily our forte. Writing this book has pushed us to expand our idea of our comfort zone and release all of our inhibitions... because we dreamers need to stick together. Not only is it important for us to support you (because we've walked in your shoes), but we recognize that it's important for us "to feel the fear and push through it."

Writing this book has been a huge blessing. It has allowed us to take a trip back to our past and revisit the path we took to get here. It has reminded us how, when, and why we fell in love with television, along with the joy and excitement we gained from some of our favorite TV shows, characters, and storylines; and how they shaped our perspectives and broadened our world. Television made us hopeful for our futures, and allowed us to see and believe that anything is possible. Most importantly, it has reinvigorated our purpose for working in the television industry—we are still dreamers whose dreams are ever-expanding. As creatives, our gift is being able to envision the worlds we want to see, and make those worlds a reality—whether they're on the page, or the big or small screen.

This book is written with an appreciation for the people who have come before us, and in gratitude and excitement for what we get to create and inspire in the generation after us. It is for people like you who are either passionate fans of television who want to write and pursue careers in TV, or those who want to pursue another career in entertainment, or anywhere else. It *is* possible, and this is our declaration to ourselves and to you—we will help you shift your beliefs to have hope in what is possible.

We are living proof that being open to infinite possibilities can open the door to our destinies. As African American children growing up in Alabama and Florida the realm of possibility was first shown to us through a television screen. We watched TV obsessively for hours on end and envisioned being part of each fictional world we encountered.

Back then, many people considered watching TV a waste of time. We were told by some, *"It fries your brain"* and by others, *"It's unhealthy to be so immersed in alternate realities."* To them we can only say, look at us now!

By 2015, we were writers on *Empire*, one of the biggest TV shows on a major broadcast network to premiere that year. We were invited to speak on panels and were featured in magazines and news programs across the country. We shared our experiences working on a television show that focused on a Black family—a *rich* Black family—written by a team of predominantly Black writers, with enthusiasm and excitement. It was incredible. We were honored to be part of a phenomenal primetime hit that garnered so much media attention. It was a complete dream come true.

It's one thing to dream big dreams. It's another to see them actualized in ways you never imagined, especially when your original dreams were already huge to most. In this book, we take a unique "She Said, She Said" approach to recalling our "sometimes separate, almost equal" life journeys and experiences as identical twins. We share our story with heart, humor, and flavor and give insight into why we believe dreaming big and expressing our authentic truths is the best recipe for success.

In essence, we believe every successful journey involves three vital steps:

Step One: Share Your Dreams Without Shame

Dreams begin as a small thought in our heads, a private vision that takes hold of us. But that vision can't actualize until we give it life by speaking it out loud or sharing it with someone else. Wild, wild dreams take us out of our comfort zones. When we first think of them, we don't have an immediate action plan or know the basic steps to achieve them. This means it will take a lot of work, persistence, and belief in our ability to accomplish the seemingly impossible to see them come to fruition. It also means it can be scary to share them with others—but it's an important step for dreamers to take.

Step Two: Ignore the Haters

When we express our dreams to others—friends, peers, and the world—we may be faced with their criticisms or concerns. However, it is not in our best interest to argue with them about why, despite their disbelief, we will achieve what we have set out to do. Think of the Lil' Wayne quote, "Real Gs move in silence." As dreamers, it's not our responsibility to defend our choices to those who don't believe in our possibilities.

Instead of proving them wrong with our words, we can prove them wrong with our actions. Their approval and their co-sign aren't necessary to achieve our dreams.

Step Three: Find Your Tribe

It takes a village to raise and nurture our dreams. We must surround ourselves with people who share the same vision, or at the very least those who share the belief that our dreams are both extraordinary and attainable. Iron sharpens iron. Finding a tribe or tapping into a network of supportive individuals who encourage us along our journey, and vice versa is essential—and if it doesn't exist, we must create our own!

As you read the following pages, you'll discover that our journey is shared across chapters that are separated into five sections. These five sections reflect the "Five Points of Story," a structure in which we learned how to write TV episodes based on a format detailed in Robert McKee's book on writing titled, *Story*. They include:

Part 1: Inciting Incident
Part 2: Progressive Complication
Part 3: Crisis
Part 4: Climax
Part 5: Resolution

So along with our journey, you'll get a little lesson on how to structure an episode of a television show.

After reading this book, we hope you will be inspired and motivated to go for your dreams. Once you learn how we—twin sisters and military brats of divorced parents—turned our passion and talents into lucrative careers as storytellers in Hollywood, we hope you will be encouraged to boldly use your voice, powerfully share your experiences, and step into your own successful, creative, personal, and professional journeys in life. We'll be waiting to read your story next go 'round...

Part One

WHEN STARS ARE BORN, DREAMS ARE MADE

Inciting Incident: *An action that creates conflict for the protagonist. It helps develop and maintain focus for the story; the jumping-off point, the starting point.*

Chapter One

HOW TV INSPIRED A DREAM IN TWO LATCHKEY KIDS

"Dreams aren't perfect. They come true, not free."
— Joey Potter, *Dawson's Creek*

JaNeika

My sister JaSheika and I are identical twins born an hour apart—okay, technically fifty-nine minutes, but still—a rarity among most twins we meet. Generally speaking, twins are usually only a few minutes apart. When people discover we were born an hour apart they always wonder: What happened?

JaSheika

What happened was our mom fell asleep for thirty minutes—during labor. I was in a breech position and needed to turn around. In the meantime, our mom took advantage of my delayed entrance into the world and took a nap.

JaNeika

Our parents, Angela Stallworth and Eugene James, met in the United States Air Force in 1980. They were married, we were born, and by the time we were two, they were divorced. It was pretty much a whirlwind. After their split, we lived full-time with our mother, who remained in the Air Force. When we were almost four years old, our mom was assigned a station in Wiesbaden, Germany, and we shipped out for the next four years.

JaSheika and I always had each other growing up. We didn't like to play outside and we didn't care too much about playing with other children because, much like on the plane ride to Germany, we were always entertaining each other. In addition to having each other, we also had a television. The TV was our babysitter. As a single mother, our mom would get up at 5 a.m. to tend to us. She'd wash us, get us dressed, then lay us in front of the TV so she could get a few more hours of sleep. Then, she'd go to work as a physical therapist at the Wiesbaden Regional Medical Center.

While we were in Germany, our grandparents on both sides—Clifford and Ethel Stallworth, and Annie Ruth and O.T. Rhodes—would videotape American television and send it to us. There was only one channel in Wiesbaden, and it was in a language we didn't speak. Our mom was young (she had us when she was only twenty-one), and perhaps that's why she wasn't restrictive about what we could watch. We'd get boxes of VHS tapes with Saturday morning cartoons like *Heathcliff* and *The Smurfs*, but also sitcoms like *ALF, Small Wonder, The Golden Girls, Empty Nest, The Cosby Show,* and *A Different World*.

That is how our obsession with television began.

JaSheika

Even though we were living in a single-parent household, watching TV allowed us to open a box that was otherwise sheltering us. Television gave us a

Television gave us a chance to see that there were so many other experiences, stories, and lifestyles throughout the world.

chance to see that there were so many other different experiences, stories, and lifestyles throughout the world. Watching it was like seeing through a window of possibility.

Our television was on the floor in the family room of our German apartment. We'd sit as close as possible to the TV, at the edge of the carpet, with our heads right in front of it. Of course, Mommy chanted the usual refrain about how we need to back away from the TV or we'd ruin our eyes. At first, we'd listen to her, but when she left, we'd sit right back in front of it.

As teenagers living back in the U.S., we spent summers with our dad in Montgomery, Alabama. He'd get so annoyed at our relentless TV watching, particularly our viewing and discussion of daytime soap operas. *"You girls shouldn't be in the house all day, wasting time watching TV,"* he'd say. He preferred for us to play sports or spend time swimming at the local YMCA. But watching soaps was one of our favorite pastimes from when we spent time with our grandmother, Annie Ruth (a.k.a. Ma). Each morning, Ma would enjoy her daily coffee and her dose of Bob Barker on *The Price Is Right*, and then we'd all watch our soap line-up of *The Young and the Restless, All My Children, Another World,* and *General Hospital*. We loved the characters of Victor Newman, Erica Kane, and Frisco Jones so much, we didn't care that it irritated our dad. Today, he doesn't complain about our TV viewing as much, especially now that he can appreciate how much it has benefited us in our careers as writers.

JaNeika

We got so much out of watching different shows and films when we were growing up, but it wasn't even a thought in our heads that we could somehow make careers out of it one day. We just knew TV shows were "cool" and made us feel good.

Our weekdays included nightly appointments with *The Golden Girls, The Cosby Show,* and the crew at *Cheers*. Our weekends were filled watching Eddie

Murphy, Dan Ackroyd, and Jamie Lee Curtis in *Trading Places*, or Steve Martin and Daryl Hannah in *Roxanne*, and even Tom Hanks in *Big*. *Little Shop of Horrors, The Blues Brothers, Splash,* and *The Wiz* were also favorites among film and TV shows that brought us immense joy at the time, not only because of the actors and the signature roles they helped create, but because of the worlds we were able to escape to and immerse ourselves in. Worlds that made us feel like we could be anything, do everything, and live anywhere.

Those worlds felt so inclusive; we could relate to everybody regardless of race or culture, which mirrored our personal experiences. Being children of parents who were in the military allowed us to grow up in a very diverse and inclusive environment. There were people of various races and cultures working and living together on every base we were assigned. We didn't recognize the distinctions that others ordinarily experience in the "civilian world," where diversity and inclusion were not as prominent. We also did not understand the uniqueness of our cultural upbringing until we were forced to face the truth of our "difference" when we moved back to America at eight years old.

Coming to America was a culture shock, and not of the Eddie Murphy/Arsenio Hall comedic variety. No, we were confronted with racism for the first time in our young lives when, after moving back home to live with our grandma in Alabama, we were informed the kids next door weren't allowed to play with *"monkeys,"* as told by their father. It was difficult going from the freedom of having friends from various backgrounds, cultures, races, and households based on genuine

We refuse to be put in a box that dictates what is or is not possible for us.

connection, to settling into the realities of American racial distinctions when people told us, *"You're Black." "We're what? No, we're Brown." "No, you're Black."* By crystalizing the definition of race in our young minds, it felt like we were being taught how to separate ourselves from other people—something we were never faced with and had no desire to do before. It was odd and uncomfortable for us. We were resistant to the rules of separation, the boxes, and the categories people wanted to place us in, which I think has a lot to do with why we are where we are today. We refuse to be put in a box that dictates what is or is not possible for us.

Chapter Two

CARVING OUT OUR NICHES

"You can do anything. You're a woman."

— Maxine Shaw, *Living Single*

JaNeika

When we were in sixth grade, our mother was diagnosed with scleroderma, which is a form of lupus, an autoimmune disease that occurs when the body's immune system attacks its own tissues and organs. She was later medically discharged from the military after serving for thirteen years. Unbeknownst to us, our lives were about to change completely. We were about to go from military children to what I call GDIs—Got Damn Independents. We no longer had the military privileges of tax-free shopping, living in base housing, and developing friendships with people from all sorts of backgrounds. By the time we began seventh grade, we had moved from Eglin Air Force Base in Fort Walton Beach, Florida to Tampa, Florida, where our aunt, Jeanetta Sheppard (a.k.a. Auntie Pat), was stationed at MacDill Air Force Base. Initially, we went to a private Christian school in Ruskin, Florida. Even though we were the only Black children at the school, we felt completely embraced, loved, and supported by all of our teachers and peers. We saw ourselves and others as just people; we didn't distinguish by race. We did start to distinguish ourselves as individuals, however.

It was hard to know who we were when all everybody saw us as was one-half of a unit.

As children, JaSheika and I had made attempts to fight for our own identities and individuality. Because our mom made us wear the same clothes, rock the same hairstyles, and share the same school supplies, at some point, I felt I couldn't escape being attached to my sister 24/7. We used to share a bedroom and one day, I'd had enough. I moved my stuff into a guest bedroom and told our mom, *"Sheika's too messy. I need my own room."* So, I got one.

We wanted to be individuals, but we also wanted to fit in with others. We were able to do that at our Christian school, but our mom was concerned that we were the only Black kids in attendance. She wanted us to grow up having a sense of who we were as young Black girls. While she was grateful for how we were treated at Ruskin, she moved us over to a public school to have more exposure to diversity.

Even after we transferred to public school, however, I often ended up being the only Black girl in my classes. Since the first grade, I had been given academic tests, and by the third grade, it was determined that I was "gifted." So, once we moved to the States, outside of the few private schools we attended, I was always placed in classes with other gifted students. I never felt ostracized or weird in any particular way for being the only Black girl in class in previous schools. But in seventh grade, when we transferred to Eisenhower Middle School in Tampa, Florida, both JaSheika and I began to feel a line of distinction between us and other kids.

In my non-gifted classes at school, like P.E. or other electives, the majority of students were African American and Latinx kids, which was dope. What caught me off guard was when other Black students made fun of how JaSheika and I talked. To them, we talked "proper"—which, oddly enough, was code for "white." As if African Americans don't or can't speak proper English. Admittedly, JaSheika and I had just moved to Tampa, so we sounded different than most, particularly the students of color. But it was challenging feeling excluded from a group of people who looked like us; I felt stuck in the middle of this weird culture clash. On one side, I felt alone and challenged about belonging amongst my white peers in my gifted classes. On the other, I felt challenged by my Black peers because of my vernacular.

Between seventh and eighth grade, it was very difficult for my sister and me to fit in with people. We felt like outsiders. When we were in Germany, we always had each other near and close. Now, we were in separate spaces at school, being challenged in very similar ways by different groups of people. One night in seventh grade, I came home crying because of this cultural identity crisis. I did not know where I fit in. I wasn't Black enough for the Black kids, and couldn't shed my Black skin fast enough for the white kids. It was a confusing time, being torn between what felt like the beats of various drummers when in reality, I simply needed to get my own drum set to march to—a lesson that would take a little while longer for me to grasp.

JaSheika

I had a completely different school experience from JaNeika. I was far on the other side of the spectrum, considered to have a slow learning disability (SLD). It takes me a little longer to process things visually, specifically when I'm reading. Because of this distinction, I was in classes with both special needs kids and badass kids. Despite being in a different setting than my sister, we faced similar challenges. Because of our military upbringing, I was used to being friends with diverse groups—white, Black, Puerto Rican, Mexican, Filipino, gay, straight, etc. At the time, I was considered "too open" for a lot of my peers, and I was called out for hanging with everybody instead of one particular group of people.

We had already moved around so much in our young lives that we had a lot of experience leaving friends and making new ones. Little did we know that our unusual upbringing would influence our lives and careers. To this day, we are women who bring people together who wouldn't normally mix or intermingle with one another.

JaNeika

At first, we were somewhat angry with our mom for yanking us out of our private Christian school and enrolling us in public school, where we didn't fit in no matter what corner we went into. One of the most difficult parts of being military brats was moving in and out of at least ten different schools by the time we were in twelfth grade. But in hindsight, we can see the role it played in how we're able to easily engage and connect with so many different people from various backgrounds today.

We became further prepared for our future when we entered high school. I decided to apply to Tampa Bay Technical High School so that I could attend a magnet program. The school had a health academy and an engineering academy that prepared students for college study in those prospective career fields. I wanted to enroll in the Academy of Health Professions.

JaSheika

Mommy didn't want us to go to two different schools. I didn't want to go to the technical high school, but my mom forced me to apply, so I enrolled in the Academy of Engineering. Our mom was always forcing one of us to do what the other was doing—usually, that meant me doing what JaNeika was doing. Initially, I was very resistant, but in the long run, attending Tampa Bay Tech was a completely life-changing experience and one I'm happy I had. The fun, the laughter, the tears, the wild moments, and the lifelong friendships formed throughout those years still serve as inspiration to the stories we tell today.

JaNeika and I were finally enrolled in separate programs and had separate friends. We even had a

Little did we know that our unusual upbringing would influence our lives and careers.

different lunch schedule. We started to experience ourselves more as individuals and were also seen that way by others. Although people still knew we were twins, we were able to carve out our own little spaces in the world.

JaNeika

Tampa Bay Tech prepared us for what was ultimately going to happen when we went to college and figured out what we wanted to do for our careers. In addition to college prep courses, the school offered access to chosen specialties in several career fields, ranging from health, engineering, and technology, to autobody, cosmetology, and business. Although it, too, was a public school, there were many different groups of people from various backgrounds who had no issue interacting with each other. The Health Academy included African-American students, Latinx students, Caucasian students, Haitians, Jamaicans—almost any culture you could imagine. It was a relief for me to discover the gifted and advanced classes were just as diverse as the classes throughout the entire school. Even though there were different groups and distinctions similar to our previous schools, at Tech we all felt and interacted as one. It was throughout this period that we formed lifelong friendships with some of our best friends, including Alecia Hill, Brandy Williams, Jennifer Reece, and Sue Ellen Carrion—friends who have supported us from the beginning and throughout all the crazy dreams we've had. It's never too early to start building your tribe.

JaSheika and I got our first taste of what it's like to break out as individuals at Tampa Bay Tech, whether it was through different sports activities like track and dance, or running for homecoming queen. I even joined the band so that I could have a second lunch period with my sister and all of our girlfriends.

Being in two separate academies allowed us to define who we were as individuals and not be known just as "the twins." It was nice to be appreciated for who we each were. In addition, that separation allowed us to be able to have two very large networks to combine.

High school allowed us to finally get to a place where we could be ourselves. We could move amongst various groups and still feel included, which gave us a sense of confidence. It felt like part of our voices had been muted previously, depending on where we were. Once we were able to feel fully accepted in high school and move freely, our voices got stronger, together and as individuals. We were comfortable with who we were, able to find our tribe, and allowed to grow unapologetically, even among the naysayers. That confidence came back to benefit us later as we started to realize and speak out about our dreams.

Throughout that period, we never let go of our love for TV. Even as we got older, we'd get so upset with our mom if she messed with the VCR and our favorite soaps didn't record. We'd ask her to write down everything that happened if we missed an episode and to purchase a *Soap Opera Digest* for us to make up for it.

We'd get on the phone the minute we were out of school, call our grandmother, and talk about what we missed. Our love of nighttime soaps was also increasing. Even though I was a very good student, I would scramble to hurry up and finish all my homework, just so I could watch TV. We had a show for every night of the week. Monday nights we watched *Melrose Place*, Tuesday it was *Ally McBeal*, Wednesday nights it was *90210*. Thursday nights we watched the sitcoms—*A Different World* and *The Cosby Show*, then it became *Living Single, Living Color*, and *Martin*. Friday nights we watched *Family Matters* and the rest of the TGIF lineup on ABC. From 8 to 10 p.m., we had a daily TV watching schedule.

We understood that we owed it to ourselves to explore the possibilities.

It used to annoy our mom because we had VCRs in every room, with our soaps ready to record. We created as much of a schedule around our TV shows as we did our studies and social activities. Our friends thought we were crazy. To us, it felt normal. We preferred to stay at home watching TV shows as opposed to going out on dates because it was so much more enjoyable. Everything we needed to get out of life, especially when it came to dealing with teenage angst, we felt we could get through a *Dawson's Creek*, *Felicity*, or *Buffy the Vampire Slayer* episode.

As teens, we had no intentions of working in television. After my first year at the health academy, I chose to work in the dental field. I was planning to become an orthodontist.

At the time, I didn't realize that I was ignoring a part of myself. The passion, love, and appreciation I had for television wasn't just some frivolous hobby I had as a pastime; it was something I thoroughly enjoyed being immersed in. A fire was being sparked in my spirit—one that doesn't just go away because more reasonable, stable occupations awaited me.

Instead of pushing our passions to the side in favor of what looked and felt satisfactory to others, we understood that we owed it to ourselves to explore the possibilities. We needed to lean into what brought us the most joy. We'd never know what was possible until we'd try.

JaSheika

My career path, on the other hand, was less clear. I enrolled in the engineering program without even knowing what engineering was. There were so many different avenues I could take, from computer engineering to practical engineering. In the last year of high school, a journalism program started in our school, where students could host and produce the morning news. I took that course as an elective.

I don't like being in front of a camera, but when I let go of my resistance, it felt so natural to produce and report the news. Whether it was working behind the camera, producing the segment we were talking about, or announcing the morning news report, I felt very comfortable in this new setting, and dare I say... enjoyed the spotlight. It was something I was able to tap into that forced me to release whatever fear I had.

Our class even helped our high school win a radio competition, because of the television show platform we used for the morning show. We used the show and the morning announcements to get the entire school to call in every single month so that we could get Tampa Bay Technical High School (TBT) representation. It worked; we won and ended up hosting a party at our school. It may seem like a small event, but it was my first foray into bringing my dream into vision, although I didn't realize it at the time.

JaNeika

Even though we kept busy with our studies and our television obsessions, we also tried other activities, whether it was the dance team, managing the basketball team, or track.

We loved to challenge ourselves and try new things. We always thought, we may not be the best at everything, or end up liking something, but at least we could say we did it. Nothing stuck quite like TV, though.

One of the TV shows that we adored watching while growing up was *Living Single*, starring Queen Latifah, Erika Alexander, Kim Fields, and Kim Coles. It was the first time we'd seen a television show led by all Black women—of different shapes, sizes, colors, and in various stages of life and love. They all had completely distinctive personalities, which was groundbreaking and unlike anything we'd ever seen before. We loved watching these young, Black, career-driven women aspiring to be successful, while at the same time balancing love and friendship.

One day, we picked up *Essence* magazine and it had an article titled, "Yvette Lee Bowser: The Sister Who Took Living Single Straight to the Top!" We learned that in creating *Living Single,* Yvette was the first African-American woman to create and run her own television series. And she was only twenty-seven years old when she did it!

We took the magazine and kept that article because it was the first time that it clicked—*Wait, what? You can do that? You can be a Black girl and be the person responsible for creating and writing all the things we love to see and watch on television?!* To learn there was this beautiful, intelligent, and incredibly funny woman—who looked like us—behind that show was so empowering. We didn't even realize becoming a creator of one's own television series was a career path, let alone a possibility for young women like us! Yvette paved the way.

Growing up, I loved to write. From journaling my thoughts to trying my hand at poetry, I had a natural knack for putting pencil to paper and seeing what evolved from my imagination. I later developed a love for writing and developing stories, specifically, stories about girls who could solve problems. My love for writing stories paid off when the Florida Writes Assessment program, a.k.a. "Florida Writes" began. It is a test given to fourth, eighth, and tenth graders to test our expository and narrative or persuasive writing skills. From the six-point rubric system of scoring, when it came to taking these assessments, I always received a six—the highest score possible. I was able to write really well, but I never thought I could make a career out of writing. When we saw that Yvette Lee Bowser did just that—for TV—both JaSheika and I stored that thought in the backs of our minds.

It only began as a thought, however. We didn't have an action plan at that time. We just thought, *Wow, we would love to do that*! But it planted a seed. That was when we first started growing our wild, wild dream.

Chapter Three

LEAP OF FAITH: HOW A VISIT TO DAWSON'S CREEK CHANGED US FOREVER

"You never know what you can do until you try."
— Miss Ellie, *Dallas*

JaNeika

As fans of the programming featured on WBTV—a network that followed the model, established by FOX, of introducing programs that initially catered to African-American audiences—we were very curious when we started seeing promos about the new series, *Dawson's Creek*. We were immediately drawn to it because it featured Joshua Jackson, an actor we enjoyed in the movie, *The Mighty Ducks*. Of course, this was going to be a hit. Plus, it was a show about teenagers–not of the vampire-slaying variety like *Buffy the Vampire Slayer*; another fave of ours. No, *Dawson's Creek* was a show about regular teenagers, which we happened to be at the time.

Dawson's Creek was a teen drama series set in a fictional northeast town called Capeside, Massachusetts, but the show was filmed in Wilmington, North Carolina. Even though the characters didn't look like us, because of our experience growing up in the military, we didn't focus on differences in race or culture. We connected to those characters and their experiences for a number of reasons. One of the girls lived with her grandmother; we were living with our grandmother. Dawson's character was obsessed with film, we were obsessed with TV. Even Capeside felt like it was a southern town, similar to the ones in which we were raised.

After graduating from high school, my sister and I attended different universities for our first two years of college. I attended the University of Florida (UF) in Gainesville and JaSheika attended the University of South Florida (USF). My best friend, Jennifer Reece, who was also my freshman year college roommate, was annoyed because I had set up two separate TVs in our dorm room—one to record our soaps, and one to watch *Dawson's Creek*. Everybody on my dorm floor knew I was obsessed with the show. I recorded it and saved the tapes. I had a whole library of tapes people would come over to check out if they missed an episode because they went out partying. As time went on, even Jennifer had to let go of her resistance to my TV obsession and join the *Dawson's Creek* fan club (or at least stop complaining when it came on Wednesday nights).

JaSheika and I turned eighteen during our freshman year of college. For spring break, we decided to go to Wilmington, North Carolina to see where *Dawson's Creek* was filmed. I was a member of an online fan forum known as Television Without Pity, and I saw on message boards that other fans would visit the set and become extras on the show. As superfans ourselves, when I told JaSheika about these fans, we knew we had to follow in their footsteps! We told our mom about our plan to rent a car and drive from Central Florida to North Carolina. She was fine with it. Again, she never really restricted us from watching and exploring things that were of interest to us. We were excited to take our first unsupervised road trip adventure. It took roughly eight hours to get there—with a few stops, here and there.

Once we arrived, we decided to play up the twin thing and use it to our advantage. We hadn't done that in years—not since we were five years old. We purposefully went out shopping for matching outfits, had our hair twisted up and curled in the same style, and funnily enough, it worked! By thinking outside the box upon our visit to the set, we garnered the attention of a few of the assistant directors as extras were selected to shoot in scenes. They excitedly declared, "Oh, we've got to have the twins in this." Thus, we eventually made one of our first TV appearances as extras in Season Four of the *Dawson's Creek* episode, "Future Tense."

JaSheika

During every part of our lives, there's been people there to help us. I like to call them angels living on earth who have guided us along our path. In this case, it was a guy and girl from Los Angeles named Edgar and Amy. We took a fan tour of Screen Gems Studios—where the show was filmed—which is where we met Edgar and Amy, two superfans, just like us. They told us where to sign up to be extras and what to do to ensure we were able to film with the stars of the show.

We signed up and spent the whole day on set. It was a dream come true for us to sit around and watch what was happening—the actors rehearsing and performing their scenes, the director giving notes to the actors after each take to pull a different performance, and the Assistant Directors managing the extras (us) and other members on set to make sure we stayed on schedule. It all felt so surreal. An added benefit, as if we needed more, was that we got a sneak peek of the next season. And because we were twins and the assistant directors were drawn to us, we were able to be extras for not just one day, but two. Mission accomplished. Getting a paycheck for doing what we would've been happy doing for free was the icing on the cake, especially since we weren't even expecting it.

Not only did we end up as extras on *Dawson's Creek*, but we also got to interact with the actors, despite having been told not to speak to them. The best moment was during our final day on set when, just as we were leaving, we saw Joshua Jackson, who played Pacey Witter on the show. Remember, he was the main

During every part of our lives, there's been people there to help us. I like to call them angels living on earth who have guided us along our path.

reason we watched the show; all we cared about was Joshua Jackson! The few times we initially saw him on set, we followed the rules and didn't speak to him or any of the actors. As we were leaving, we finally got the courage to ask if we could take a picture with him. He said yes! We chatted a bit about our favorite music, where we were visiting from, and said our final goodbyes. That last moment made our entire trip worth every cent. In the end, our trip to Wilmington took about seven days total. Three out of those seven were spent on set.

JaNeika

That was one of my favorite moments ever. What we didn't know at the time was that seeds were being planted for our futures. I've come to realize how hard it is to know what you're capable of accomplishing until you're able to see yourself in it—visualize, if you will. It's important to have some sort of perspective of what your dream would actually look like.

We always knew that we loved TV, but to go on the *Dawson's Creek* set and see what it was like for a show to be in production, to witness all the different roles that people played in producing it, was a dream come true. It was amazing to see how the actors could be shot by three different cameras, in twenty-plus takes, just for one scene! And then when those scenes were cut together, they ended up being only thirty to forty-five seconds of footage. This was the world of television and film. We felt privileged to get a sneak peek into a world we'd only dreamed about, and could now finally see what it looked like.

JaSheika

Edgar also told us that the writers weren't there on the set—they were in LA. We learned that writers should have distance from the set. That planted another seed that maybe one day we'd move to Los Angeles.

We also learned that people on the set are led by the director; the assistant directors (ADs) keep everything running. The ADs are watching the clock, making sure scenes are finishing on time, and ensuring that the extras are there. Then there are production assistants, who are the runners, getting everything the cast, director, or ADs on set need. These were the people we interacted with the most during this time, but they are only a few of the most essential roles on the set of a TV series. A shoot day could last as long as fourteen hours, and while we only see the people in front of the camera, there are hundreds behind it, making sure the shot of a scene is perfect, from the Director of Photography (DP), cameramen and women, the grips (camera support), hair and make-up artists, etc. They say it takes a village to raise a child. Well, it takes a generous collective to produce a successful TV show.

Having that experience opened us up to what was possible. Without seeing what it was like to produce a TV show, we would not have been able to have a fully formed idea in our brains as to what it would look like for us to have careers in the field. We still didn't know how we were going to get there, but now we had something to strive for. We knew from being extras that acting was not for us, but we also knew there was a role for us in writing or production. We returned to college after that spring break knowing we had to change course in our studies.

Chapter Four

CHANGING COURSE

"We're women. We have double standards to live up to."
— Ally McBeal

JaSheika

From a young age, we're often encouraged to figure out where we're headed in life. If my sister and I were to give our younger selves a piece of advice today, we would say: *Be open to possibility.* What we've come to realize is how important it is to change course a couple of times in life and not feel bad about it. An expectation we've often felt put upon us was *not* to shift. The notion instilled in us by society is that we are to decide early on who we want to be or what we want to do, then never change our minds. If that were true, I wouldn't have the career I have today.

When I initially began college, I enrolled as a mass communication major at the University of South Florida (USF) in Tampa. I stayed home, living with my mom while attending school. I worked a part-time job and gave my entire paycheck to her each week. Eventually, I started to resent feeling like I was living for other people. I wanted to stop being such a people-pleaser. I knew there was a TV program at the University of Florida in Gainesville (UF), so I applied to transfer there after my first two years at USF.

I was accepted into the College of Journalism and joined my sister two years into her on-campus life in Gainesville. By then, JaNeika had established her own friend groups, sisterhoods, and social schedule that encompassed an entirely new and different lifestyle than the one we had when we were under our mom's roof in Tampa.

JaNeika

When I was in high school, I had already decided to have a career in dental health. Foolishly, I applied to only one school for college: University of Florida (UF). Thankfully, despite my limited scope of applications, I was accepted. At the time, I wanted to eventually go to dental school, so I enrolled as a nutrition major. I got straight A's my first semester of college and as a result, I became part of the inaugural class of Bill Gates Millennium Scholars. That scholarship supplemented my entire undergraduate education. What a blessing Bill and Melinda Gates were to me!

In school, I joined several social and cultural organizations and took part in leadership roles and responsibilities that broadened my overall collegiate experience.

I tried to put myself out there and create my own identity outside of my sister, and then BAM! She shows up one day and joins the College of Journalism to study TV! My whole world was rocked. There I was, suffering through math and science classes—that I sometimes enjoyed, yet mostly hated—and my twin was studying what we've loved our entire lives—TV. While she was having a great time discussing shooting commercials, working in production, and learning to write news, I was completing physics labs, enduring statistics exams, and trying to figure out how to drop out of calculus.

The idea that I would eventually go to dental school meant a great deal to my dad. He wanted me to stay focused on that vision. He didn't have a problem with

> What we've come to realize is how important it is to change course a couple of times in life and not feel bad about it.

JaSheika studying telecommunication, but for me, he was clear... *"Dentistry is where it's at!"*

JaSheika

A distinguishing factor that probably made our dad less freaked about my choice to study telecommunication was that I was very financially responsible. At the time, JaNeika was not, and unlike her, I didn't depend on our dad the way she did. So, in his mind, he wanted to be certain that after school, she'd get a steady job or at least a decent paying job, so she wouldn't have to depend on him as much. I'm sure there are a number of students with huge ambitions whose parents share the same fears our dad once had.

JaNeika

But I'll be honest, I resented him for that. I couldn't understand why my dad was okay with JaSheika doing TV, but wouldn't even let me consider switching to it. It felt like an untenable double standard. I remained a nutrition majoring honor student for as long as I could, but eventually, I questioned why I was doing that to myself. I liked most of my courses but I loved TV more. JaSheika was thriving and having fun in her major. So, for the first time in our lives, I followed my sister—instead of the other way around—and changed my major.

In joining the "J-School" (UF's College of Journalism) as a telecommunication major specializing in business, it felt like a weight had been lifted off of me. As the gifted child—the Gates Millennium Scholar—I found myself following a very linear, professional track, even though my heart wasn't in it. This was the first time I acknowledged that. There was true freedom in that truth—the freedom to go after what I wanted and what my heart most desired, professionally.

In both my and JaSheika's experiences, there is a lesson. Our hearts were filled with the most joy when we prioritized living for ourselves, were honest about our true wants and desires, and felt free to pursue goals that felt true to who we were and wanted to become. From that point on, never settling in pursuit of our passions became our primary standard.

My mom—always a free spirit—didn't mind my change in course, while my dad pushed back. For him, it was almost like an arrow went through his heart. Up until I started working on *Empire* in 2015, he still talked about me going back to dental school at some point. He had poured all this money into supporting my lifestyle and supporting my studies. As difficult as it was to decide to transfer all my studies into the College of Journalism from health and nutrition, it was one of the best decisions I've ever made.

I felt so relieved and grateful to be in the same college as JaSheika and to take classes with the professors whom she had already met. JaSheika was a telecommunication major with a minor in production, and I became a telecommunication major with a minor in business. We ultimately believed that one day we would work together; I'd have the business mindset, she'd know all the production details, and we'd be good to go. Of course, nothing is ever that easy.

Part Two

SETBACKS THAT SET YOU UP

Progressive Complication: *A turn in the story that makes a character's life more difficult.*

Chapter Five

YOU TAKE TWO STEPS FORWARD, I'LL TAKE TWO STEPS BACK

"People waste their time pondering whether a glass is half empty or half full. Me, I just drink whatever's in the glass."
— Sophia, *Golden Girls*

JaNeika

JaSheika and I were very much in a rush to get out of college in exactly four years. Once college was over, we were also very clear about what we wanted to do. We just had no clue how to get there. So initially, I moved from Gainesville back to Tampa with my mom for a couple of months. That was a horrible decision; I went from being a seventeen-year-old teenager who lived under my mom's roof all my life, to now being a twenty-one-year-old adult who couldn't stand living under her rules, now that I'd had a taste of independence.

I was in a weird juxtaposition of being independent—and then suddenly not being so independent—while also having to figure out how to pay bills and contribute to my mother's household. It was uncomfortable. I ended up moving into an apartment with my best friend, Marlon Furlongue, who also felt uncomfortable being back at home post-college. We had an affordable two-bedroom, two-bathroom living arrangement, but I had to start working a nine-to-five job for the first time ever.

I got up every weekday morning and headed to St. Petersburg to work for Cox Target Media's Valpak as a media consultant. That was code for selling coupon packages to local businesses featured in the monthly Valpak envelope, but I liked the idea of putting "media consultant" on my resume. It was a cool title, especially for someone trying to figure out how to get into writing for TV. I also loved the idea of getting out of college and making a $30,000 base salary with the potential of making so much more in commissions. But I hated soliciting people for business to grow my business.

I would come home so tired every night, with very little time and energy after my commute and workday. I'd basically come home to eat dinner and get ready for bed, then the cycle would start all over again the next day. It was something I could not fathom doing for the rest of my life, no matter how much potential wealth I could build in the process.

I began to resent the fact that I didn't take my time in school. I could have been sitting in classes for an extra year, collecting financial aid like the rest of my friends, not having to worry about bills, or going to a nine-to-five job. Why had I been in such a hurry to graduate? It felt like I had rushed out of school to go pay bills. It was clear this was not the life that I wanted to live; it was never part of my dream. I knew I had to get away from a monotonous routine. I wasn't in a dire situation, but I wasn't happy with my station in life and that made me realize that the dream was not something that was going to all of a sudden just happen to me. It was something I had to go out and get for myself.

What it came down to for me were these questions: How big is your tolerance for risk? How much can you lean into your faith that you will ultimately be provided for and taken care of? How much do you believe that everything happening is for your benefit? My fear of failure was not greater than the fear of not being satisfied with my station in life. I feel one has to outweigh the other; either I would continue to be unhappy and settle for less than the dream, missing out on what my life was meant to be, or I would step out on faith and know that the internal feeling of discomfort I had was for a reason.

We feel that God, the universe, or whatever higher power one subscribes to pushed us to step outside of our comfort zones. It forced us to leap toward what we felt called to do.

What I've come to know about myself is that, as a creative, I need variety. I am so grateful I'm in the business I am now because, while there is a lot of uncertainty, that uncertainty comes with an extreme amount of excitement—which is what my sister and I thrive off of as creative people. There is no monotony in TV; every day is completely different. There's a joy that comes out of being able to dream about an idea and watch as that idea comes to fruition. There are always obstacles along the way, but ultimately, we enjoy troubleshooting and navigating our way through them. Whether it's in production, in the writer's room, or dealing with casting or music, we always have to troubleshoot, but we find great fulfillment and achievement in doing it—every single time.

JaSheika

After graduating from college, JaNeika moved in with Mommy while I came home and moved in with our Auntie Pat. I was so grateful for that opportunity because living with her helped me eliminate debt while I worked toward becoming an adult. Although I now had a degree in telecommunication, I was still unclear about the path I would follow toward my career.

I started working at Time Inc. as a telemarketer. I worked there for a year, which also helped me get out of debt, but still—I wasn't fulfilled. It felt like I was spinning my wheels and my spirit was being crushed because I wasn't doing what I felt called to do. I was also in a relationship that I had been in since I was sixteen. After graduation, our mom hinted that I should consider marriage to my boyfriend at the time, but he made it clear he didn't know who he was going to marry. Those words woke me up. I paused: *Wait, what do you mean you don't know who you're going to marry?* I thought we had made an unspoken commitment to marriage. For me, it was never a question.

That moment was a huge turning point for me. We ended our relationship, and that became a step in my journey that allowed me to move forward. I realized I needed to take action to do what I wanted to do. I applied to two different programs: film school at Florida State University (FSU) and the ABC Studio's Production Associate program in Los Angeles, California.

I was invited to interview for film school, but fear kicked in. I was so afraid of being unprepared and not good enough, to the point where they wouldn't accept me. I drove up to Tallahassee to do the interview but when I got there, I just sat in the parking lot. I didn't go to the interview. I shut down even the opportunity to go to film school so that I'd only have one option—the program in Los Angeles.

A couple of days later, I got a notification that I had earned an interview for the production associate program at ABC. *Thank God*, I thought, because I had just killed my backup plan. I flew out to California with my mom. *This is my chance. This is so cool*, I thought. I was excited. I had the interview and although I was very shy, I felt I'd done really well. I went back to the hotel that night and learned I was the first runner-up. Although they liked me, I didn't get the job. I was crushed.

I cried to my mom, who told me to call the woman who coordinated my interview, Jean Hester, and ask for feedback. I called her and she said, *"Your interview was really good, it was just that some other people we interviewed have more of the personality we are looking for. You did really great though, and since you are our first runner-up, if something happens with another candidate, we will call you in."* I said *"okay"* and we flew back to Florida.

I'd be lying if I said I wasn't somewhat hurt, a little depressed, and completely devastated when I came home. I'd always trusted that when things don't work out in ways I expect, they simply are not part of God's plan. The difficult part is that I was so sure the Production Associate's program was a part of God's plan for me.

Within two weeks, however, I received confirmation on what that plan truly was. I got a call saying that things didn't work out with one of the original candidates and was told I could take the person's place if I moved to Los Angeles. Within the next two weeks, I moved. I only had two thousand dollars in the bank and had to ship my car. I still had a little bit of debt, so my budget was limited but I was fortunate and quickly found a roommate with an apartment minutes away from my new job at ABC Studios. With the support of my mom and Auntie Pat, my transition to California was almost seamless.

So, there I was, all by myself, starting a new job without knowing exactly what I would be doing! I was under the impression I'd be working for ABC News in Los Angeles. Negative. I was working for the studio—at the time called Touchstone Television—that produced primetime shows on the ABC network and many others, like *Felicity* on The WB. By the time I started the job, they had just finished shooting pilots and were getting ready to launch *Desperate Housewives, Grey's Anatomy*, and *Lost*; it was a golden era for the ABC network and its studio. Essentially, it was a dream job, yet at the time, I had no idea I accepted what would eventually lead to my dream position.

JaNeika

When I look back on my experience working for Valpak, I can see how it prepared me for all the pitching I'd have to do in my career. As writers, pitching is a superpower we're always forced to use; we pitch ourselves to get the job, we pitch in the room to land a story for characters, we pitch full versions of our episodes to be approved by the showrunner so we can be commenced to script, we pitch to a studio or a network when we try to sell a TV show. We're constantly pitching and selling. So, unbeknownst to me at the time, Valpak was the perfect training ground for the skillset I would later need to successfully work as a TV writer.

When I had the job, though, I couldn't wait to get out. While JaSheika was applying to film school at FSU and to the ABC Associates Program, I applied to every graduate school that I could. I felt it was time to pursue and focus on my dream. I applied to Emerson, Syracuse University, USC, and UCLA. I ended up getting accepted to Syracuse University's S.I. Newhouse School of Public Communications—a yearlong program that allowed me to get a master's degree in television, radio, and film. At last, I was finally getting closer to my dream.

Chapter Six

A DIFFERENT WORLD: JASHEIKA TO LA

"Relax, relate, release."
— Whitley Gilbert, *A Different World*

JaSheika

While working at ABC Studios as a production associate in my year-long apprenticeship program, I covered phones for an executive who oversaw *Desperate Housewives*. However, I was also getting exposed to all facets of television. When I first got the job, I thought I wanted to be a producer. But really, I was afraid to admit what I really wanted to do—write. Fear is a constant thing that creeps up on me.

I didn't have any idea of what it took to be a TV writer, so I started exploring other fields. Along with the production associate program, I did an internship at a management company. I thought being with people who manage actors and talent and get scripts would put me on the creative side of the business. I didn't realize I was already getting the best opportunity to grow in the direction of my dreams while working at ABC Studios. It turned out to be the best school I've ever had; it was so far advanced in terms of the access I had to the reports, budgets, and production experiences.

But at the time, it appeared to my naïve eye that all the executives did was manage budgets and tell producers yes or no. They felt like babysitters and therapists combined, managing people's personalities and expectations on set and off. It seemed extremely taxing and very unfulfilling, creatively. Witnessing that dynamic completely turned me off from the idea of producing.

I shadowed Angela Nissel, one of the writers of *Scrubs*, for a day, while they were shooting her episode. I got to see what it was like on set and meet the actors (who were really funny), but I also saw the difference between filming a comedy and a drama. *Scrubs* was being shot in an abandoned hospital in the Valley—Hollywood, but not Hollywood because they were in their own little world. It was a much more relaxed environment than what I'd seen at the studio. Filming comedy, not surprisingly, resulted in a lot of laughter both in front of and behind the cameras.

I used to think that comedies, since their scripts had shorter page counts than dramas, would be easier to write. It was a gross mischaracterization of what it takes to write scripts. Comedy, although it takes place in such a shorter amount of time, takes just as much effort as drama, sometimes more. Comedy writers have to establish who the characters are in fewer pages, whereas in drama you get twice as long to set the stage. A comedy is usually only half an hour of air time, meaning about thirty pages (give or take), whereas a drama is an hour of TV (sixty pages, give or take).

As I watched them shoot and read the *Scrubs* script while sitting beside Angela, I also saw the actors take the liberty to change things. They were allowed to improvise. I asked Angela if she was okay with the fact that they weren't saying exactly what was on the page and she said she was. That was my first experience of learning how writers can collaborate with the actors. Because she was flexible and not too attached to the words on the page, whatever the actors were inspired to bring to the table could be used instead. This is not always the case on every TV set—some writers and showrunners are very particular about cast members remaining true to what is written on the page. However, this was the experience on *Scrubs*, which didn't seem to hinder the show creatively, but instead enhanced the fun of the series.

Angela not only allowed me to watch her in action with the director, the actors, and other members on the production, she also gave me a copy of her script and walked me through how the story of the episode came about. She helped me track where they were in the series because the episode wasn't slated to air for a few months. She told me about the writers' room, the makeup of it (I believe at the time she was the only woman of color in that writers' room), and what she enjoyed about being in a comedy room. Just those few hours of being on set with her inspired me and allowed me to see firsthand how it was possible to become a writer.

At the time, I was taking an extension writing course at UCLA. I had written a couple of scripts with my sister personally, not professionally. We were new to the craft and I was not yet polished enough to understand that in TV, you don't have to be so tight with words. Now, as a result of my experience—and what I first learned from Angela—I'm not super attached to my words if the intentions behind them are still there. I recognize and understand that actors say what comes naturally to them in character. If they're not saying exactly what I wrote, it's not an offense to me or my script, it's more a reflection of how my words inspired them to live those words and create something true to their character. Writing and producing is about collaboration throughout the entire process.

As a production associate, I was a very diligent worker, so much so that I was the one who came in and helped relieve the assistants to the executives whenever they needed to go to lunch, take a break, or were out sick. I was so good at what I did that all the executive assistants wanted me to cover whenever they were out. Even the senior VP of the studio would have me, his substitute assistant, cover his desk because he trusted me. Soon, I even ended up covering for the assistant to the president of the network.

Having access to executive rooms was an important step for me in my career. Being able to see how things work at that level created a vision for me to be in the same space as these highly successful people. I had ideas of who these people were, but then being in their office at their desk, listening in on phone calls, I got to hear how business gets done. And after spending so much time around these powerful executives, I quickly realized they put on their pants one leg at a time just like we all do. Even though they are making big moves, they're just like the rest of us.

Seeing how people in executive high-level positions operate showed me things I could apply to my own work ethic. Witnessing so much, I'd see people operate in integrity, and I'd see people operate outside of integrity. To see who did what and where they are now is eye-opening.

In any position I've held, I've always approached the job from a place of consideration: What would I want from someone working for me in this role? When I worked for executives at ABC Studios, I would imagine myself as an executive and think about all the things I would need from my assistant in order to do my job. With that in mind, I'd show up to work fifteen to twenty minutes prior to my start time. I'd check voice messages before my bosses arrived. I updated their calendars and laid out their schedules for the day and I'd prep and organize the office to their liking.

Doing this may seem like a lot, but it was a small effort in comparison to the huge reward it generated setting the tone of my, and my boss's, overall day. I did this daily, with gratitude and joy, because deep down this job was a dream come true. I had access to scripts, budgets, and other highly confidential information surrounding productions of various hit shows. I was able to watch executives manage and lead as they put out fires, navigated personnel, and managed the budgets and expectations of creators with grand ideas for their shows. I was grateful to have this access and wanted to soak up as much information as I possibly could.

I would often cover for an executive named Victoria LaFortune, who at the time covered *Desperate Housewives*. When the program ended, one of the executives referred me to a spot at Sony to work as a PA on *The King of Queens*. I took the job, even though it was such a distance away from where I lived. It wasn't long before I realized my experience was more advanced than the job required. The job required me to fill out receipts, get lunches and breakfasts, and clean the kitchen.

I wasn't above doing those things. However, I had learned so much during my time at ABC that I found myself crying while driving home from work one evening because I wasn't able to use my knowledge and experience the way I expected. I found myself praying to God, *"If this is what you want from me, I will do it. I don't know how long I can take this, but if this is the path you have set for me, I am willing to do it."*

It was five or ten minutes later that I got a phone call from Victoria's office. She had been on vacation when I left and was upset to find out I was gone when she returned. Her assistant told me she had something for me. Victoria set up an interview for me to be the producer's assistant on *Desperate Housewives*. I agreed to the interview right away. I stayed on *The King of Queens* for two weeks and moved on to *Desperate Housewives*. *The King of Queens* hadn't even started production yet, but when I gave my notice everyone was excited that I was leaving to go work on the new hit show, *Desperate Housewives*. A highlight of my career is that I've always worked on hit shows, and I'm very grateful for that. I am forever grateful for Victoria, an executive who saw my potential and gave me that referral.

I left *Desperate Housewives* after a season (I wasn't asked to return... more on that later) and went to *Dexter*, where I worked in accounting. I was in accounting simply because it was a position that became available; I still hadn't shared with anyone what I really wanted to do and didn't know the steps I needed to take to get staffed as a writer. Part of me was afraid I would lose my job if I expressed my passion and said there was something else I wanted to do. The other part was worried I wasn't good enough to be a writer.

I had a lot of subconscious doubt to work through that was a result of questioning my ability to write a script by myself. I didn't understand at the time that writing was a collaborative process. I also had a perfection complex. I felt that when my words touched the page, they had to be flawless, as opposed to understanding that writing involves a lot of rewriting. These are not unique fears.

In Hollywood, there is a common perception that you only get one shot to make a good impression. For example, I mentioned that after my first season working on *Desperate Housewives* I wasn't asked to return. In hindsight, I believe a huge part of my not being asked back was because I wasn't clear on the duties and responsibilities of the job and made one error too many. In this fast-paced work atmosphere, most top-level executives need their assistants to be 1,000 miles ahead of them. I was learning while on the job and still unclear about my place in production. Hollywood doesn't give you much time to figure things out; you either learn or you don't. And if you don't, you're done. It was a lesson learned, but one that unfortunately, I'd have to relearn later.

There may also have been another subconscious observation that kept me from visualizing myself in the writing role. I didn't see many people of color in the writers' rooms. I saw a few women, but not Black women. I don't know if that fact intimidated me—my sister and I had certainly been the only people of color in a classroom before—but I do think it may have affected my confidence and added to my belief that I had to perform above 100% to prove myself.

As I was working on *Dexter*, I befriended the executive producer's assistant, Diana Marrone, and we bonded over the Carly and Sonny characters on *General Hospital*. One day I told her I wanted to be a writer and she said, *"Oh, JaSheika! I wish you would've told me sooner. I could've gotten you in the writers' room. My boss loves to mentor people."* That was a lesson in learning to speak up and not be afraid to put what I wanted to do out in the world. From that moment on, I started being more open about my dream, speaking it out loud and sharing it with others.

Around that time, in 2007, I also became secretary for the Organization of Black Screenwriters. A few years later, I was in a writer's program, the Guy Hanks and Marvin Miller's Screenwriting Program, which supported African-American writers. As part of the course, we went through the history of African-American contributions to TV and cinema.

Early on in my career, I thought, *"I just want to be known for being a good writer. I don't want to be known as a writer who is only able to tell certain types of stories."* As someone who loved *Living Single, A Different World,* and *Martin*, I also loved *Dawson's Creek, Ally McBeal*, and *90210*. I saw universal qualities in those shows that didn't have to do with race. I wanted people to notice that my sister and I could write shows about everyone and everything; we didn't want to feel pigeonholed into one particular type of storytelling. Our life experiences were so diverse and inclusive, and we wanted to bring all of that to our writing.

Two things shifted my perspective on that. One, I realized that if I, as a Black woman, couldn't tell my own stories, then who's going to? I saw how important it is for me as a Black female writer to tell stories about the Black female experience because there were very few others doing so at the time. Who else was going to initiate telling important stories that reflect upon us? Stories that represent people like myself, who don't often see themselves on television?

Growing up in Tampa gave us a window into a melting pot. Hollywood, when we finally got there, felt much more segregated in comparison. There aren't many writers in this industry, period. The Writer's Guild has maybe 15,000 members but only 8,000 or so are active in the whole country. And of those 8,000, only 300 or fewer are African American. So, there's a sense of responsibility to tell our stories and tell them right, and to be the ones that are championing and pushing for our stories to be told.

The second turning point came in 2012 when we met Erika Alexander, who played Maxine Shaw on *Living Single*, at a party. She asked, *"What do you guys do?"* We said, *"We're working to become writers."* She grabbed our hands and said, *"Hurry up, Sisters, because we're waiting on you."* She told us she and her peers—specifically Black actresses—were looking for us to tell the stories and create the characters they could portray. I never felt so convicted about how important it was to unabashedly, unapologetically tell our stories until then.

I realized that whether someone is Black or not, he or she would still be able to relate to stories portrayed by Black folks—at least that is my hope. Universal human experiences in our stories could be applied to their own experiences. Everything that JaNeika and I write, regardless of a characters' race, sexuality, or gender, our main goal is to show their humanity. We can write for the evilest character in a series, but viewers are going to see that villain's humanity and find something in which they can relate.

JaNeika

We've come to understand that our race, culture, background, vast experiences—interpersonal and otherwise—are the superpowers we hold that embolden us to tell stories that connect with people. Yvette Lee Bowser, the creator of *Living Single* who later became my close friend and mentor (more on that later) has always told me, *"Write what you know."* A lot of the stories she has told are based on her personal, real-life experiences. The initial belief we held, that to become successful writers we had to move away from our own experiences, was false.

Instead of trying to avoid using our experiences as women of color and trying to prove that we should be included in telling all types of stories, we realized our strength is actually in sharing our unique experiences coming from our specific point of view. Those qualities are what got us onto *Empire*, which became one of the biggest television series in the world in terms of audience reach. That show is what helped us touch so many different people cross-culturally; the fact that it told a story about a Black family is something that I'm very proud of having had the opportunity to do.

Chapter Seven

HIGHER LEARNING: JANEIKA TO SYRACUSE

"Sometimes it's the smallest decisions that can change your life forever."
— Felicity Porter, *Felicity*

JaNeika

When I applied and got accepted to Syracuse University in 2004, I thought I was going to attend graduate school in New York City. *Bright lights and big cities that never sleep*, I thought. I didn't realize that upstate New York is completely different from *Sex in the City*, New York—it's in the middle of the state and it's freezing cold and gray most of the year. As a southern girl from Florida, I didn't know what it was like to experience seasons throughout the year, particularly winter. I hadn't seen snow in a good decade.

I drove up to Syracuse with my dad, and just like JaSheika had no clue she was working for ABC Studios and not ABC News, I did not realize until orientation that I was enrolling in a private institution. It was going to be expensive! You would think that throughout the process of applying to the school and registering for classes this gifted student would have noticed that. Nope. On day one when I began my master's program at Syracuse, I had no clue how I was going to pay for attendance for the rest of the year.

I had to get a job almost immediately. I started working in the edit bays at the S.I. Newhouse School of Public Communications, helping film students check out equipment and reserve editing rooms. But I still didn't earn enough money to pay for school. Because of the circumstances I suddenly found myself in, I began to get grounded spiritually. Working and studying at the same time was more difficult than I expected it to be. It was an experience that, thankfully, I had not had prior to this because of the scholarships I acquired as an undergraduate.

I found a church home in Syracuse, called The King's Healing Room. I began attending regularly with my girlfriend, Nicole Small, who is still one of my good friends to this day. We both found ourselves in very similar positions—going to graduate school yet not necessarily having the means to be able to put ourselves through the full master's program. One day our pastor, Reverend Brian K. Hill, Sr., told me to write down three things I wanted to achieve that year and to bring that list to him the following Sunday.

I thought about it for the entire week. One of the first things I wrote down was that I needed money in order to survive and stay in school. I was also suffering a massive broken heart at the time. I remember waking up one day and calling my sister, bawling. There was a three-hour time difference, so it was the middle of the night for her when I called, but for me, it was in the wee hours of the morning on the East Coast. The way I was crying that night, she thought somebody had stabbed me. So, another one of my wishes at the time was to be over the breakup. The third wish was that I wanted a job immediately after graduation. I could not afford to be a struggling artist after attaining what amounted to a $40,000 master's degree. I wanted to be in a position where I'd be working under somebody who could help move me forward in my career, immediately.

What I didn't realize is that by becoming very clear about what I wanted to achieve and writing it down on paper, I began the process of manifesting every single goal I wrote down. I qualified to receive a student loan, so one of the wishes came true almost immediately. Eventually, I got over my heartache, thanks to one of my best girlfriends to this day, Mioshi Hill. She reminded me there would be plenty of other heartaches throughout my journey: *"One dude doesn't get to stop your train to success."* Later, I told one of my professors, Richard Dubin, that I needed a job after graduation. Together, we strategized about how I could achieve my third and final goal.

Dubin suggested we create an independent study project. I came up with a thesis study on the "African-American Female Influence in Television." Dubin is a former TV writer who worked with Ralph Farquhar on a show called *Frank's Place,* among others, and knew a lot of influential Black women in Hollywood. The goal was for me to do a study where I would interview a few of the women he knew—and other Black female creatives in the industry that I would cold call—so that I could begin building relationships that would help me acquire a job as soon as I moved out to Los Angeles. I interviewed writers such as Winifred Hervey, who worked on shows like *The Golden Girls, The Fresh Prince of Bel-Air,* and created a show called *In the House* starring LL Cool J. I interviewed Meg DeLoatch, who worked on *Family Matters* and created the television series *Eve.* I interviewed executives at United Paramount Network (UPN) and Lifetime, including Kim Fleary and Kelly Goode, as well as several Black female casting directors, including Winsome Sinclair and Eileen Mack Knight.

I interviewed a prominent Black female publicist, who was running her own public relations firm at the time— the now very successful, award-winning director, Ava DuVernay. In 2005, as the head of her company, DVAPR, Ava shared with me that she didn't think there was a glass ceiling for creative Black women. She said there were a number of Black women showrunners as well as Black women working on dramas, not comedies, and as the visionaries behind shows. This was at a time when Shonda Rhimes, creator and executive producer of *Scandal* and *Grey's Anatomy,* was coming into her

What I didn't realize is that by becoming very clear about what I wanted to achieve and writing it down on paper, I began the process of manifesting every single thing I wrote down.

own as a powerhouse Black female drama showrunner, creating opportunities for Black female actresses to lead in one-hour dramas on network television.

It was enlightening to discover that so many different positions held by women of color helped contribute to the development and success of such incredible television. It was a life-affirming experience being able to meet and interview African-American women who worked in the business and discuss their wide range of contributions to the world of television. JaSheika and I were very clear and specific in our focus on becoming TV writers. That was going to be *our* contribution to the world of television.

The final person I was able to interview for my thesis project was Yvette Lee Bowser, the creator and showrunner of the TV show, *Living Single*. That series was one of the shows that began our obsession with TV, and it was the article featuring her in *Essence* magazine's December '94 issue that inspired our dream to pursue writing for television as a career. It took a while for me to gain access to Yvette during my thesis interviewing period. She was running a show on UPN at the time that premiered when JaSheika and I were seniors in undergrad. We thoroughly enjoyed watching Yvette's new show called *Half & Half*; a series about two half-sisters who didn't grow up together, but were living in the same apartment building as adults.

Yvette was hard to get in touch with, initially, because her assistant at the time, a lovely woman named Colleen Quinn, was exceptionally good at her job as a gatekeeper. I had planned a whole trip out to Los Angeles in the spring of 2005 to interview several women and wanted to meet Yvette in person, but Colleen helped prolong an in-person appointment—mostly because of time and scheduling issues. A showrunner's life is extremely busy and their time is one of their most valuable commodities. It took me six months to actually get the interview scheduled... by phone. When I finally got her on the phone for our scheduled call, a month after my trip to Los Angeles, it felt like it was kismet. We connected instantly.

Living Single is a show I will always love and appreciate for celebrating Black women and female friendships unlike any other series I've watched to date.

During our first call, I was able to share with Yvette how much the show inspired me and my girlfriends while we were growing up. From the signature catchphrase *"Khadijah don't need ya"* to Terrence "TC" Carson singing "My Funny Valentine," the show introduced me to musical moments and moments of love and laughter that I aspired to embrace within my own friendships. As a young, Black woman growing up in a '90s kind of world, I was so glad to have my girls—and *Living Single* to watch each week.

Yvette and I talked about TV... for three hours. I didn't realize how much I could run my mouth! Luckily for me, she never indicated she didn't have time for such a thorough and enlightening conversation. She was in it with me, and I didn't realize how big of a deal that was until I later took into account that she was married, had two young children, was running a show, and was responsible for the livelihoods of 150+ people who worked on that show. She is an extremely busy and accomplished woman. To take three hours out of her day to have a conversation with me—a young fan from Tampa, Florida—seems insane in hindsight.

It was so cool to finally talk to her and realize, in a sense, that she was just like me in terms of our taste and sensibility for the TV we loved. At the end of our call, she asked what my plans were. I told her I planned to move to Los Angeles in a few months after graduation. She let me know that if I had any follow-up questions for my thesis, I could simply email her. We hung up, and I immediately called my sister. *"You'll never believe who I just got off the phone with,"* I squealed. For the next twenty-four hours, I was in awe of what took place and couldn't believe I had Yvette Lee Bowser's—a woman I had idolized since I was thirteen—email address. I had to use it.

The next day, something in my spirit told me: *"It's now or never."* I emailed Yvette and told her that after graduation I'd be looking to complete my credits at Newhouse with an internship in Los Angeles. To my surprise and incredible delight, she responded and said I should give her office a call when I got to Los Angeles. The lesson: Never be afraid to shoot your shot, especially when it involves a dream job opportunity.

It was a dream come true talking to Yvette, an exhilarating, full-circle moment. I thought back to when I saw the article in *Essence* about the first African-American woman to create and run her own television show. That moment lit a match, and talking to her on the phone was like putting lighter fluid on the flame that would ultimately fire up my career in television.

One of the first pieces of advice she gave me as a writer was to *"Write what you know."* An interesting thing I learned from our first call was that all four of the lead women in *Living Single* stemmed from Yvette. From Khadijah James (the mama-bear, boss chick best friend) to Sinclair James (her wistfully optimistic and aloof cousin) to Regine Hunter (the bougie, wig-loving, princess with a penchant for finer things) to Maxine Shaw (the pro-woman, legal eagle badass)—there are characteristics in each of these women that represent pieces of Yvette. It's a testament to how we as women are not just one thing. We're so many different things. The beauty in embracing all parts of ourselves is that we can take the greatness within, and go off and create something as timeless and exceptional as *Living Single* to encourage and inspire women for decades.

I suddenly realized the divine timing of everything. Had Yvette been able to meet with me in person during my trip to Los Angeles, we probably wouldn't have had as long of a conversation or connected in the way that we did. At that age, I was so impressionable and nervous to talk to women who I considered heroes. Since I had already interviewed several women before talking to Yvette, I wasn't as nervous. Instead, I was clear about what I wanted to discuss. It felt like providence was leading me to everything that I wanted and needed. I didn't know where I'd ultimately be led, but I was showing up for it.

Chapter Eight

WEST COAST IS THE BEST COAST... FOR US

> "Excuse me. My job depends on me getting in there to do my job. You know what your job depends on? Me getting in there to do my job... Sometimes just gotta show 'em who's boss."
>
> — Mona Thorne, *Half & Half*

JaNeika

I finally moved out to Los Angeles. The dream had seemingly arrived. The first thing I did was reunite with my sister. It was crazy driving around Burbank and seeing Bob Hope Drive, and for some reason thinking about *The Price is Right* when I got there. *"Can you imagine what Ma* (our beloved grandmother who passed away in 1999) *must be thinking, seeing us out here in Burbank, going to visit the set of The Price is Right?"* I asked JaSheika. We agreed: She must think we "made it." Los Angeles felt like the first week or two at college when everything is brand new and full of exploration and excitement.

The next thing I did when I arrived was call Yvette. She kept her word and immediately set me up with an appointment to come to her offices at CBS Radford Studios, where *Half & Half* was shooting. Yvette and I connected on the phone for my thesis study, but we still had to make sure we gelled in person. I was able to pass the litmus test and assure her that I wasn't a crazy person—at least enough that I could start interning for her and the show.

While working for Yvette, I began to clearly understand the defined roles of production staff. I'd never worked on a television set before, so I got to see everything her job as a showrunner entailed. She wasn't just a writer; she was the ultimate producer in charge of overseeing every department in production, while managing the show's regular cast members as well as studio and network expectations for deliverables of scripts and final cuts of each episode. When things were great, Yvette was responsible, and if ever things were not so great (hardly ever), Yvette was responsible. I could now see that being a showrunner meant taking on everything—both the good and the bad. Yvette was managing a multi-million-dollar business for the studio, which is essentially what being a showrunner is today.

A television showrunner is usually, but not always, the creator and head writer of a TV show. The showrunners manage the day-to-day overall production of a series, from pre-production to post-production. All of the department heads report to them. They have the final say on scripts, but they also act as a liaison between studio staff and production staff as well as with the network. It's a lot of responsibility. That's why they get paid big bucks to do it. It's a very stressful, yet fulfilling position to have.

Showrunners oversee every single department on the set. So, I wasn't just somebody interning as Yvette's assistant. In addition to that, she had me working in the writers' room, in the production office with the accountants and coordinators, on set with the director and ADs, as well as with the casting directors and costume designer.

She wanted me to see what it was like to be responsible for all of these different departments. I remember being on set when she checked to see how Mona's hair (Mona was one of the characters in *Half & Half*) was for a scene. If it wasn't right for a character's mood, she would have them redo the hairstyle. She had the final say on anything reflective of the characters in the series, from not only the words on the page but down to every single look on the stage.

In a similar way to how JaSheika was able to work in various jobs on the studio side, I was able to work in these different departments on the production side of the show. I now realize that was great preparation for one day running our own show. Yvette knew that, as a young woman with the same aspiration as hers, it would be important for me to understand what the people working for me had to do. Working in those different departments allowed me to see what everyone else was bringing to the table and how to respect everyone's role and passion, while also maintaining a vision for what it was that I wanted. The best showrunner is somebody who can inspire other people to get excited and to create their best work that is in line with the showrunner's vision.

Mona's character on the show had what was called "The Mona-Logue," an interactive blog in which "Mona" would answer online questions in real life from fans of the show. It was a part of the series, and some of the questions and answers were read in the episodes. Yvette allowed me to write and answer questions from this character's perspective for the blog she maintained, which I thought was incredible. She allowed me to pitch jokes, as well as give notes and feedback on scripts. I felt so involved. One of the greatest moments in my career was being an intern at twenty-three years old, working at Yvette's desk and picking up the phone one day, and having someone say, *"Hey, can I speak to Yvette?" "Yes, who can I tell her is calling?" "Oh, this is Bernie, baby, Bernie Mac."* The Bernie Mac Show shot a couple of stages around the corner from our offices. Another highlight was when Cedric the Entertainer called my cellphone looking for Yvette. I had no idea where he got my cellphone number, but it was pretty cool.

I was excited about finally being out in Los Angeles, moving toward the dream. The prayer (or third wish) I had asked God for when I was in Syracuse was finally coming to fruition. I felt like I was where I was supposed to be, at the start of my career path.

Initially, my dream was to become a writer. But through my experience interning with Yvette, I started filing away the idea of becoming a showrunner. I realized that not all writers have a vision for a show; some turn to the showrunner and say, *"Tell me what it is that you want."* As storytellers, JaSheika and I have always had such a strong vision when it comes to what we want to say character-wise, story-wise, and emotionally—the story points we want to hit and have connect with viewers. Because we are cognizant that we are very much like our TV viewers, we want to provide what they want to see. It became clear to us early on when we started working that to have the final say in actualizing the specific vision we desired, we would have to become showrunners.

But because it was such a complicated position, I was aware we'd have to pay our dues before we could get there. As an intern, I wasn't getting paid. Interning is not for the faint of heart. An unexpected medical discharge settlement my mother received from the military is what made it possible for me to live and work for free until I transitioned from being an intern to becoming Yvette's assistant, which took three months. God is good, that's all I can say. I went from making no money to making $650 a week, then to $850 a week–which may seem like a lot, but Los Angeles is not a cheap place to live. That money did not stretch very far; there were many frugal times for us in the early days.

We would have free groceries, however, because we worked on shows where all meals on set were provided. And entertainment-wise, we could go to premieres or get tickets to the movies for free. During Oscar season, we could attend free screenings of all the movies campaigning for nominations.

Roughly seven months into my time as an intern working on *Half & Half,* The WB Television and United Paramount Network merger happened. Two television networks were being cannibalized into one. They went from UPN and The WB and became the CW. During this transition, the network downsized the amount of programming by half since there were fewer time slots for the number of shows on both networks. Decisions were made on which shows were to stay and which were to go. Twenty shows on two separate networks were ultimately reduced to ten shows on one, brand new network. *Half & Half* was one of the shows that did not survive for placement onto the CW's new lineup. Unfortunately for us and the fans, Season Four ended on a cliffhanger.

Yvette is such a hard worker, though. She put her blood, sweat, and tears into running and producing an amazing, incredible show. Before we got the official word *Half & Half* was not being picked up, I remember working with her for hours as she put together an exciting pitch for season five. She almost broke the entire fifth season in her house over the course of two weeks, which is something that you don't usually do until you get your writers picked up for the next season.

Throughout that time, I realized how emotionally draining it is to try and keep a show on the air. In the end, no matter how hard we worked and how great Yvette's Season Five pitch was for the characters of Mona, Dee Dee, their moms, Spencer, and Adam— it didn't matter. The CW picked up three shows from UPN and canceled everything else.

It was heartbreaking for Yvette, but also eye-opening for me. I learned that, as a showrunner but also as show staff, you need to be prepared for major disappointments and changes in direction at all times. More importantly, however, was the life lesson that life still goes on after rejection. You can survive that type of rejection or denial in this business and continue to thrive. I feel like there was a purpose in me witnessing that, as difficult as it is for creative people to let go of something they're passionate about, there is a certain level of detachment from the outcome that is necessary in order to survive in this business long-term.

It's important to expect the unexpected, to be flexible and open to things shifting and changing, and to be okay with that. Being able to adapt to sudden shifts and changes in course is a skillset that I did not know I needed to become a successful writer. But it's

It's important to expect the unexpected, to be flexible and open to things shifting and changing, and to be okay with that.

something that I had to experience on my ten-year journey to the writer's room to be able to thrive there.

So, with *Half & Half* suddenly canceled, I went from being Yvette's intern to becoming her full-time personal assistant. The person who created one of my favorite shows and ran several shows from the time she was twenty-seven up until this point, was no longer running a show. So, what did my job suddenly look like? As her personal assistant, my duties sometimes included picking her kids up from school, helping with grocery shopping, forwarding business calls, and helping her prepare pitches and decks as she developed new TV show ideas. It was completely different from when I'd first moved out to Los Angeles and began as an intern. As Yvette used to correctly joke—it was not at all what I expected to be doing with my $40,000 master's degree. But it was what I asked for. I wanted to have a job as soon as I got out of graduate school so that I could move forward with my career, and that's exactly what this job was— the beginning of my career in television. There were certainly some moments, though, where I questioned my choice to pursue this dream.

Something I had learned at this point was how important it is to get specific about what you want out of the vision of your intended dream. Too often, we overlook the details about what our dream accomplishment specifically looks like once it is achieved. How do I feel now that the dream is accomplished? What do I wake up to every morning as a result? Does the dream include work on the weekends? At night after 6 p.m.? Get specific because on the path, there will be valleys, as well as peaks, and there will also be times when your finances, your social commitments, and your impending deadlines impede upon your creative process all at once.

When I first had a head-on collision with a moment like this, I questioned whether I was really built for this pursuit. The more these moments occurred, the more nights I found myself falling to my knees at night and crying out to God in prayer, asking if this is where I was supposed to be. Although I was working and earning a living, the doubts I kept having weighed heavily on my soul.

And that's the untold truth about being a creative working in the entertainment business—the doubt is constant. It does not stop once you've hit specific goals or reached a certain level of success in your chosen profession. To this day, there are times when I still question whether I'm good enough. The difference between now and yesteryear is that I've learned to push past and dismiss that question almost immediately when it is posed.

Chapter Nine

GO HARD OR GO HOME

"But, if indeed our paths ever did cross, it's up to you to remember me."

— Dominique Deveraux, *Dynasty*

JaSheika

While we were working hard for our pennies in Hollywood, our friends were buying houses, getting married, and taking all the steps in life in which we lagged behind because we were in pursuit of our dreams. From the beginning, JaNeika and I made a pact with one another that if, within ten years, we were not working as professional writers, we would consider taking that long trek back home. The caveat for us was that within those ten years, we had to exhaust all of our resources, or as we'd often say, *"Go hard or go home."*

JaNeika

Although I was learning a lot throughout my early years striving to become a TV writer, the length of time it was taking to reach that goal did start to take a toll on me. I had been a gifted student; I was an overachiever throughout my entire educational career, and I had come to Los Angeles and gotten a job almost immediately. I was living in LA, working for my idol on the show I grew up watching in my final years of college. I was in pursuit of my dream career. Even after *Half & Half* was canceled, I continued to grow as an aspiring writer. While learning how to write, develop, and create television, it was instilled in me that as Black women, we have to work twice as hard to get half the results of our peers and counterparts.

After six years of interning and working as Yvette's assistant, the job ended in 2011. I was twenty-nine years old. It was devastating because, at the time, I didn't have any idea what my next steps were. Unemployment was something I had never experienced. But here's the interesting thing about California: unemployment has a nickname, "fun-employment" is what it's called, particularly for people who work in Hollywood. Because of the freelance nature of our jobs and how often people go in and out of work, unemployment benefits often help people living and working in Los Angeles survive.

It was terrifying to fill out unemployment paperwork, but it was something that I had to do. It would pay me about $450 a week, which was less than what I earned when I first started working in the business and pretty much impossible to live off of in Los Angeles. I had worked for six years to have around $10,000 total in unemployment funds, which seems like a lot, but that can be burned through pretty quickly. Again, it's very expensive living in a city like Los Angeles.

The longer my unemployment lasted, the scarier it got for me because the funds were diminishing rapidly. My sister was working at ABC and we had so many friends in various positions all around town that I figured I could send out my resume and get another job quickly. *It shouldn't be that hard to get a job as a showrunner's assistant, right?* That was my initial thought. *I did it once, I could certainly do it again. Right?*

Wrong. I was unemployed for seven months. During one of the most difficult periods of my life, it was frustrating to make daily phone calls to my mom and cry about how I'd spent so much on two degrees—a bachelor's and a master's— only to *not* have a job. I'd call my dad and beg him for money every few weeks just to keep up on most of my bills. He was very good at not saying *"I told you so,"* and always provided what I needed without question, even if he didn't have much to give. In the back of my head, I felt guilty because I knew he probably just wanted me to attend dental school instead of pursuing what felt like a fruitless endeavor in entertainment. He would always say, *"You know... there's always a plan B."* In my head, there was no such thing as a plan B–at all.

Unemployment forced me to put my ego aside. I was humbled, heavily, throughout that period. I grounded myself and got on my knees in prayer with God on a regular and consistent basis. Although it was a very difficult and scary time for me professionally, it was one of the best times for me spiritually, as I took that time to strengthen my relationship with God and truly surrender unto His will. I felt like the Lord was preparing me for bigger trials I would later face. Hopefully, this period was a simple pre-test, so that when the time came, I'd be able to pass the real test of my fortitude in this business with flying colors.

I started to question my choices. I started to question my dream. I started to question my direction and whether or not everything I did was all for naught— beginning with going to grad school and spending $40,000 for one year of study. That one year of school cost more than my entire undergraduate education. As a woman of faith, a lot of times when I go through hardships, I question: *What is the lesson in all of this?*

My saving grace was the creative space that opened up for me during that period. Because I wasn't working, I had to put my money where my mouth was. I said I wanted to be a writer, so I thought, *Well, finally nothing is distracting me from doing what I say I want to do—write!* Having a job and working in the field was even a distraction from achieving the dream at times because I got so caught up trying to make money to pay bills, I didn't have time to put substantial effort into my creative pursuits.

As a creative, I can admit we're sensitive beings when it comes to our creative processes and duties and responsibilities in our lives that often interrupt them. In order to function, we must create, but in order to be in a position to create, we must pay bills. In the past, all too often, the hours and mental energy required at my jobs left me way too tired to come home at night and write. Although PA gigs and assistant jobs in TV put you exceptionally close to the positions you may want to be in, working ten or more hours per day in any number of these jobs is exhausting—mentally, physically, and emotionally. For most creatives, not being able to create leads to depression. Depression often prevents us from creating.

It's a vicious cycle we don't even realize we're in while in pursuit of our dreams. Receiving unemployment pay meant I no longer had a job to distract me from creating.

I wrote a couple of pilots by myself and developed some story ideas. Even though my sister and I planned to write shows together, I needed to prove that if she was able to get a job and write by herself, I could do it if I needed to, as well.

We were convinced that getting staffed as writers was what we were called to do. We did not see any other opportunity for ourselves outside of that—mostly because we didn't want to. Similar to my dad, folks in Los Angeles would often bring up what their plan B was in the event their dreams didn't pan out. JaSheika and I, however, have never had one. I don't know if that's a good piece of advice for others to follow, but I know it was good—and is what worked—for us. If you don't see any other option, you don't allow your brain to be open to an escape hatch. We trained our brains to truly be focused on what we envisioned for ourselves—writing for TV, come hell or high water.

When we first moved to Los Angeles, we met a lot of people—transients from other cities and states—who had dreams similar to ours. We formed various friendship circles, but as years went by, we'd notice people packing up from Hollywood and moving on. They'd get married, have kids, and return to their home states. They decided they weren't going to do what we were doing anymore. They weren't able to live off $800 a week and felt they needed "real jobs." We constantly heard, *"I'm leaving, I'm transitioning. I've got to go do something real."*

For those of you reading who happen to be dreamers, be aware and mindful that sometimes you're going to hear people refer to what you do as if it's some sort of fantasy—something that's not tangible or real because they aren't able to achieve it. That mindset is not something you have to internalize or take in as you're on the path to actualizing your dreams. In fact, it's a mindset you should work very hard at blocking so it doesn't permeate your own. The truth is, sometimes people's dreams change, and that's okay. Those initial dreams were not real for some who were once in your circle, and because they weren't, they shifted. However, just because someone else's dream has shifted, doesn't mean the same has to be said of yours.

Our advice to those of you who are still dreaming is to move as if the dream has already come true. I used to cringe when people would suggest that to me, but it's one of the most genuine pieces of advice I've ever received and can be applied to every single area of your life. When I pray as if I am already moving in a dream realized, that dream feels that much easier to experience when I finally achieve it. But make no mistake—achieving our dreams has not come easily. It took a long time for us to have breakthroughs. We had many moments of tears, anger, and frustration along the journey, but what kept us going was maintaining the belief that our present circumstance did not have to define our future reality. There are times when you're going to want to fall apart and cry—and we did! But after we allowed ourselves to have those moments, we'd get up and head right back on our path toward the dream.

As our friends began to get married, have children, and buy houses, we'd look at ourselves and say, *"We want those things, too."* We just didn't want to sacrifice what we were striving for professionally and suddenly feel like we had wasted years of our lives pursuing dreams left unfulfilled. We wanted those things, but we also wanted to have our careers. In all honesty, there were moments when we'd wished we aspired to have careers that were more stable and less volatile than those in the entertainment industry. While friends back home were earning PhDs, becoming doctors, lawyers, and moving forward in professions with very clear and direct paths, we were on a much more wayward path that at times could feel very rocky, scary, and uncertain.

On the flip side, when our friends back home would visit us in "Hollywood," they'd presume we were leading these fabulous, luxurious lives because we worked in TV. Yes, we could take them to live tapings and introduce them to famous actors on sets, but sometimes I couldn't make my car payment. Yes, we could hike up to the Hollywood sign and run into a famous hip-hop artist at a local restaurant, but my student loans were in deferment. Financial abundance, stability, and a sense of knowing that the goals JaSheika and I pursued were indeed going to happen was not part of the reality we lived, and our closest friends and family were completely unaware of that. It made those times even more difficult than they already were.

In those initial ten years, there was a question mark around everything. *Am I doing the right thing or am I wasting precious years of my life?* I was in my twenties and not taking the time to do much else outside of work, including dating. Whether or not I would have a future spouse was unclear because I was so narrowly focused on becoming a writer. Getting staffed was of the utmost importance to me. I thought, *If I get staffed as a writer and make enough money to cover my bills and pay off my loans, everything else will fall into order. Then, I can focus on dating and eventually building a family.* In that order, so I thought, but much like the stories we've learned to write for television, the best ones aren't quite as linear.

It wasn't until later that I realized how important a life filled with balance is, in addition to the dream. In my twenties, it was all about one thing—getting a seat at the table in the writers' room. As I got older and witnessed my friends hitting various life stages, it became clear to me that my own dreams encapsulated so much more. In addition to wanting to have a successful career, I wanted to have a husband and I wanted to have children and become a mother. Once I acknowledged

> *It wasn't until later that I realized how important a life filled with balance is, in addition to the dream.*

this to myself, it became imperative that my dreams fall in place quicker than ever.

One of the first steps we had to take to get placed in a writers' room was to build our writing portfolio. When JaSheika and I started in the business, we wanted to be comedy writers, so we wrote comedy spec scripts. A spec script is a writing sample of a TV show that is currently on air. Your spec, or speculative script, is one you write on your own that you're not pitching or writing to sell—at least not initially. The purpose is to show that you're capable of stepping in and writing an episode of television in the voice of the show.

A key distinction we learned about being a staff writer versus being a showrunner is that staff writers are not hired to write in their own voice—they are hired to write with their showrunner's voice in mind. The showrunner is looking to read the staff's scripts and not have to make too many changes. Staff writers who are adaptable to the voices of various showrunners generally have better opportunities at getting staffed on other shows.

As we wrote spec scripts and pilots over the years in the hopes of becoming staff writers, JaSheika and I applied to writing programs with all of the major networks—Nickelodeon, ABC, Disney, Warner Brothers, and many more. In 2009, we took part in USC's Guy Hanks and Marvin Miller's Screenwriting Program, which opened up a lot of doors for us.

Although we didn't make it into a writing program for one of the major networks for many years, we do recognize the importance of talent development and inclusion programs and the access they create. If at first you don't succeed, it's a good idea to apply to these programs again. Persistence is key and recognizable in applicants who are committed. Fun fact: After years of not being accepted into Nickelodeon's Writing Program, JaSheika and I served as judges for the program years later. It just goes to show you that if you don't succeed, it doesn't mean you won't find success in other, unexpected ways.

The script that ultimately got us into the program that helped launch our careers was *Immediate Family*. It's a story about a young girl whose father dies from a freak accident and in the aftermath of his death, she and her mother discover he had three additional children who happen to attend the same school. When we wrote that story, we felt there were a number of kids experiencing similar situations with blended families, as opposed to the nuclear family generally presented on television. We were interested in telling stories about universal experiences that often go untold. Telling that story is what eventually got us into the FOX Writing Intensive Program in 2015, which led to us getting staffed on FOX's hit series, *Empire*.

Looking back at our lives, and the variation in our journeys when compared with those of our best friends and professional peers, we learned to stop comparing. There was purpose in every single pitfall and triumph we've had along the way. From the rejections and job losses, to the program access and finally getting staffed at *Empire,* I wouldn't take our ten-year career journey back for anything. The struggle we endured along the way is what has helped build character in us as professional women.

Sometimes huge risks are required for the reward of fulfilling your dreams.

JaSheika

When I hear people say they want to write, but their actions portray a different story (a.k.a. they have no scripts to back it up)—my advice is this: It's one thing to say you want to write, but it's another to make sacrifices in order to complete a script. If your dream hasn't manifested, you should reevaluate how you go about trying to achieve it.

For things to change in your life, whether financially or personally, you cannot be unwilling to take risks. Sometimes huge risks are required for the reward of fulfilling your dreams. When you are resistant to change you may as well tell the universe, *No! I don't want what you have to offer me!* When it comes to manifesting your dreams, a decision has to be made. You either go hard... or go home.

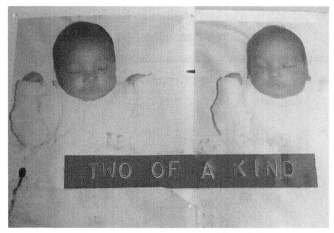

(JaSheika James and JaNeika James - 2 days old)

From the womb to the world!

(JaSheika James and JaNeika James – 10 months old)

Same fit, different colors—always!

Fifth Grade Academic Team. All-Star on a gifted team of students at Oak Hill Elementary School on Eglin Air Force Base.

(JaNeika James)

Planting seeds. First-time visit to the set of *Dawson's Creek* in Wilmington, North Carolina.

(Mommy, Granddaddy Cliff, JaSheika, Lisa, Uncle Tyrone, Grandma Ethel, Auntie Pat, JaNeika, Cynthia, and Daddy)

With family after graduating from the University of Florida.

UNIVERSITY OF
FLORIDA

College of Journalism and Communications
Department of Telecommunication

2081 Weimer Hall
PO Box 118400
Gainesville, FL 32611-8400
(352) 392-0463 Fax (352) 846-2899
telecom@jou.ufl.edu
www.jou.ufl.edu/tele/

Date: February 12, 2003

To: Graduate Admissions Office – Boston University
College of Communication

From: James Babanikos

Re: Janeika Nashae James

Janeika asked me to write a letter of recommendation for her to get into your graduate program, and I am only too happy to comply.

Janeika was my student in an Advanced Writing for Electronic Media class I taught here in the fall of 2002. The course is designed to provide a thorough understanding and overview of the principles of scriptwriting, and to learn to apply these principles through practical exercises in various formats: commercials, sponsored and corporate videos, radio and television documentaries, as well as fictional works. Janeika performed very well in that class, but what really impressed me about Janeika was her focus, her enthusiasm and her determination to create and produce television programs that address significant social issues.

Janeika loves television, and recognizes the power of that medium. Her long-term goal is to develop dramatic series and sit-coms that make a positive impact on society, especially in terms of race relations. She recognizes that television has come a long way in breaking down stereotypes, but feels more needs to be done. She thinks it's necessary for visible minorities to be involved making the programs, and not just playing in them. These are lofty goals, especially for someone coming right out of school. But everything starts with a dream, and with a lot of hard work, experience and maturity, there's no reason why Janeika's dream can't come true.

Janeika has quite a bit of imagination and some great ideas. She's now learning how to better articulate those ideas and translate them for the screen. Janeika has the "vision," and the stories she wants to convey are relevant.

Janeika is also interested in the business side of this industry, and is minoring in Business here at UF. In the long run, she wants to create programs, as well as produce them. This is certainly ambitious, but she's intelligent, dedicated, hard-working and responsible. A graduate degree in communication can be of immense benefit for her to achieve her goals.

Yours Sincerely,

James Babanikos, Ph.D.
Associate Professor
(352) 392-0442

Grad school letter of recommendation from Professor James Babanikos

March 6, 2003

The Peter Stark
Producing Program

Lawrence Turman
Chair

Kathleen L. Fogg
Assistant Director

Janeika James
111 SE Sixteenth Avenue #0306
Gainesville, FL 32601

Dear Ms. James:

I regret to inform that you were not selected for The Peter Stark Producing Program for Fall 2003. You will receive official notification from the University later. Yours was a serious application, and I'm sorry for your disappointment.

Twenty-Five students, plus a short waiting list, were selected and are being notified separately. Each application was reviewed completely and carefully, with every possible effort to be fair. Decisions are final. We do not re-review.

Reasons for non-acceptance

We weigh the entire application. No single element eliminates anyone except, by University Policy, a **composite** (Verbal & Quantitative sections only– Analytical does not count) **GRE score below 1000**, or **GPA below 3.0.** This year, the average GPA was 3.45, and average GRE was 1245, though high grades and scores by no means ensure acceptance. With space for only 25, there's not room for everyone who meets the requirements. About one applicant in eight secured a class or waitlist place.

Often those with lower scores ask us to "not count the GRE." With applicants from diverse studies and universities around the world, the GRE is a necessary comparative indicator. I promise we would not make you suffer the GRE if we could disregard the scores. Please understand--an impressive resume, or strong recommendations, do not take the place of the required GRE Scores. These things are needed in addition to the required scores.

For International students, language is significant factor in acceptance. We do not use text books, so students must completely understand the lectures in order to compete for required grades. Shades of meaning are critical to communicate in this business, thus strong, idiomatic, conversational English is absolutely essential to succeed. We simply can't risk a place in The Program on a student for whom we have any question about language skill.

Our applicants are excellent students from top schools. All have impressive accomplishments and recommendations. Acceptance is competitive because there are more applicants than spaces. You were a fine candidate and would likely be accepted to many other graduate programs.

Reapplication

University of
Southern California
Los Angeles,
California 90089-2211
Tel: 213 740 3304
Fax: 213 745 6652
e-mail: pstark@usc.edu

If you feel your application didn't represent you fairly, or have improved GRE scores, language skills, or experience, please apply again next year. To reapply, request an application package from The Stark Office in August. We

And still I rise… even through moments of rejection.
Keep pushing!

NEIKA,

HERE IS THE MONEY FOR YOUR TUITION.
I KNOW YOU WILL ROCK IN SCHOOL.
I LOVE YOU ALWAYS

BRANDY

When JaNeika couldn't afford grad school, our best friend, Brandy, gifted money that allowed completion of a master's degree, and continued pursuit of the dream.

Thanks to people who believed in me very early on, I was able to pursue and complete a master's degree in Television, Radio, and Film from the S.I. Newhouse School of Communication at Syracuse University.

JaNeika's very first studio badge on *Half & Half.*

"Through this journey of discovery... ": JaNeika's First-Time working on a TV show, UPN's *Half & Half*.

(Nicole Small, JaSheika James, Dana Cooper, and JaNeika James)

At the "Pajama Jam" Season Four Premiere Party of *Half & Half*.

That's So Raven spec script

FADE IN
INT. SCHOOL HALLWAY-MORNING
RAVEN and EDDIE walk down the hallway and head towards
their lockers. EDDIE pulls out a bullhorn to make a
dramatic announcement. RAVEN is too busy studying a list
in her notebook to notice.

                    EDDIE
                  (excitedly)
          Boys and girls, may I have your
          attention please!

The STUDENTS stop and give attention to EDDIE> RAVEN,
however, is too engrossed in writing in her notebook to
take any notice.

                    EDDIE
          TODAY-IS-THE-LAST-DAY-OF-SCHOOOL!

EDDIE breaks out into a dance as the students celebrate the
end of the year.

                    EDDIE
          No more school!

                    STUDENTS
          No more school!

                    EDDIE
          We so cool!

                    STUDENTS
          We so cool!

EDDIE notices that RAVEN hasn't joined in on the
celebration. He heads back over to RAVEN.

                    EDDIE
          Rae did you hear me?

RAVEN ignores EDDIE as she continues to jot down in her
notebook. EDDIE picks up the bullhorn.

                    EDDIE
          I said—RAE DID YOU HEAR ME?

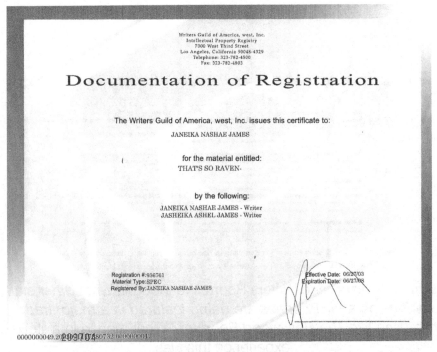

First time "writing" a spec script. We had absolutely no clue what we were doing.

"If at first you don't succeed, dust yourself off and try again." — Aaliyah

(JaSheika James, LaTonya Croff, Olivia Reyes, Sabrina Warda)

On vacation, in Greece, after JaSheika's option on *Revenge* was "not renewed."

(Radha Blank, Jamie Rosengard, Ilene Chaiken, Attica Locke, Joshua Allen, JaNeika James, Carlito Rodriguez, Danny Strong, Eric Haywood, JaSheika James, Malcolm Spellman, Ayanna Floyd, Ingrid Escajeda)

Empire Season Two Writers Room. We thought: *What other staff writers on a hit TV series are being featured in a major trade magazine like The Hollywood Reporter?* What a once in a lifetime experience this was.

(Lisa, Daddy, JaSheika, Mommy, Gary, JaNeika, Auntie Pat, Uncle Tyrone)

(Sue Ellen Carrion, JaSheika James, Sabina Frederick, Jennifer Boatwright, and JaNeika James)

(Sabina Frederick, Sue Ellen Carrion, Jennifer Boatwright, JaNeika James, and Mioshi Hill)

Our wonderful family and BFFs at the premiere screening of our first *Empire* episode.

(Empire Writers and Trai Byers)

(Empire Writers and Grace Byers)

(Empire Writers and Jussie Smollett)

(Empire Writers and Gabourey Sidibe)

(JaSheika James, Diane Ademu-John, Dianne Houston, JaNeika James)

(JaSheika James, Rhyon Nicole Brown, Diane Ademu-John, JaNeika James)

(Diane Ademu-John, Serayah, JaNeika James, JaSheika James)

(JaNeika James, Jussie Smollett, Millicent Shelton, Diane Ademu-John, JaSheika James)

Dreams really do come true! In Chicago, on the set of *Empire*.

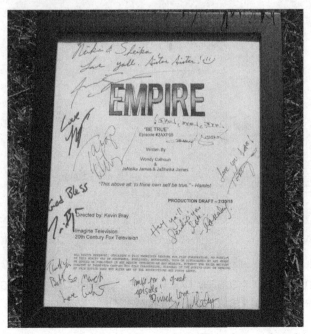

Cast-signed script of our first *Empire* episode.

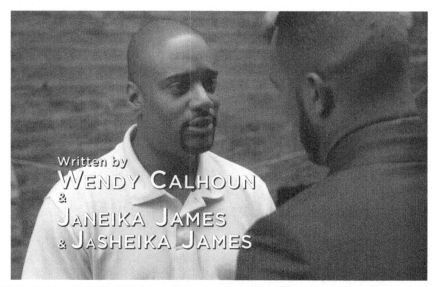

First "Written By" Card on *Empire* Season Two, Episode 205 titled, "Be True".

First time JaSheika saw her name appear on an episode of television; *Revenge* episode 218, "Masquerade".

JaSheika's first network produced script of episodic television on
Revenge.

JaSheika with her former boss and the creator of *Revenge*, Mike Kelley. He gave me my first script in TV!

JaSheika wrote the DVD extras as a writers' assistant on *Revenge*, the first season.

JaSheika and Gabriel Mann aka Nolan Ross on the set of the *Revenge* DVD extras segment.

JaSheika James

Age:19

Year:Junior

Major:Telecommunication

Hometown:Tampa, FL

Goals:To increase GPA & become extremely successful in the T.V. industry

Hobbies:Going to the Gym, TV

JaSheika wanted to share this photo as a reminder and a testament to the power of declaration. I wrote this in my junior year of college at 19! Look at my goal aka dream!

(Eric Haywood, JaNeika James, Bevy Smith, JaSheika James, Joshua Allen)

Speaking on the "Empire Talks Back" Panel at the 2015 American Black Film Festival Panel in New York City.

(Brandy Williams, JaSheika James, JaNeika James)

At the premiere viewing of JaSheika's first *Revenge* episode.

(Binta Moncur, JaSheika James, Sue Ellen Carrion, JaNeika James, Alecia Hill, Jennifer Boatwright, Nancy Cruz, Sandra Quinones)

With Best Girlfriends at *Empire* Screening Party in Tampa

(Auntie Marion, Auntie Pat, JaSheika, Uncle Junior, Kattie Stallworth, Mommy, Daddy, Lisa, JaNeika)

Empire Screening Party in Tampa

(Daddy, Lisa, Jerrell, Jacqueline, Mommy, Shon, Auntie Pat, Uncle Tyrone, JaNeika, Uncle Raymond, Uncle Ricky, Shan, JaSheika, Auntie Marion)

A Family Affair at the *Empire* Screening Party in Tampa

(Carla Waddles, JaSheika James, Yvette Lee Bowser, JaNeika James)

Always meet your idols!

Part Three

NO WAY OUT

Crisis: *The point at which the main character is forced to make a decision.*

Chapter Ten

NAME IT AND CLAIM IT

"I don't want to be down anywhere with the rest of you. I want to be special and I'm going to be."

— Erica Kane, *All My Children*

JaSheika

After working in post-production for four years as a Post Production Coordinator at ABC Studios (ABCS), I got to a point where I realized that I was either going to have to invest in that field and make it a career as opposed to a job, or I was going to move on to what it was that I really wanted to do. My boss, Celia Hamel, would say, *"This industry is built for the youth, and you're not getting any younger."* I either had to jump off a cliff and take that huge leap of faith toward writing, or I was going to stay exactly where I was, then turn around and start walking back down that mountain.

At the time, I was working a comfortable nine-to-five job with benefits at ABC. I didn't take any work home. I didn't work on weekends. I left that comfort and stability to work as a freelance writer's assistant, with no guaranteed income. I decided to walk away from a job making almost fifty grand a year with benefits, paid vacation, and overtime to follow my dream to work in a writers' room. Some called it running away from "job security." It was a fork-in-the-road moment where I made a decision that looked crazy to everyone but me. There's a certain level of conviction and faith that one must have in their dream in order to pursue it, regardless of how it looks to people who are not on the inside.

It was the summer of 2011 and we were in the midst of pilot season. Pilot season is a period where networks pick up and shoot scripts of new series to consider for their fall season's schedules. I remember reading a script at that time called *The Revenge of Emily Thorne*. That pilot script would later turn into the hit ABC series, *Revenge*. As I read the script, I was able to visualize everything that was happening on the page down to the last detail. I told my sister, *"Oh my God, I have to work for the guy who wrote this script."* The creator of the show was Mike Kelley. He's an amazing writer, and I knew I needed to work for somebody like him in order to grow from being a good writer to become a great writer.

One of my really good girlfriends, Jess Pineda, who was also a production associate a couple of years after me, was working in creative development (the department that oversees and helps develop pilots). This is where networks come in handy. Through her, I met Joe Fazzio, a brilliant writer and one of my great friends to this day. At the time, he was also Mike Kelley's assistant. Joe was cautiously excited because he didn't know what was going to happen with Mike's show. However, if it went to series, he would be promoted to staff writer.

JaNeika and I were encouraging him, convinced it would go to air because it was unlike anything we'd seen before. It was like witnessing magic in the making, and it all started on the page. Joe was so taken aback by us. He said, *"I love you guys. I need to be hanging around you all the time because you're so positive."* The show was picked up a few weeks later. I was on a cruise when I got an email from my friend who connected me to Joe, telling me *Revenge* got picked up and they were looking for a showrunner's assistant. I submitted my resume for the position and met with Nne Ebong, the creative executive who helped develop the pilot. Nne then referred me to Mike Kelley, the creator and showrunner of the series.

At the interview, I remember saying to him, *"Everything you put in the script is what's on the screen... how did you do it?"* He jokingly said, *"I call that 'director proofing.'"* I call it brilliant. Mike wrote every detail—everything you see, every action the characters take—into the script. He was so clear about his vision and what he wanted to see on the screen, and it was executed flawlessly.

When the conversation got going, Mike was like an open book. I sat across from him and asked him questions about how he got his start as a writer, as he sat back in his chair. I think he appreciated my admiration and respect for his script and the completed pilot that was delivered because he then told me, *"Nne referred you and I don't take her referrals lightly."* I ended up getting the job—not the showrunner's assistant job, but a job as writers' assistant, which was far better. I love Mike for this. To this day, I still email him or send him cards and thank you notes because, if not for him, I wouldn't be where I am right now.

Being a writers' assistant allowed me to be in the writers' room, where I could see the process of breaking story from scratch. For *Revenge*, there were several people in the room creating that show, and they did it in a bubble. Being able to witness and experience that was better than any class I could have taken.

Since the show was only picked up for a certain number of episodes, there was no guarantee that it would not be canceled. I just had those few months of guaranteed freelance work, with a salary that had been cut in half after I left post-production. I remember one of the other writers saying, *"Has anybody thought about what they're going to do if the show doesn't work?"* I remember thinking, *Oh my god*. It didn't even cross my mind that the show could fail and I would be out of a job again.

JaNeika

Meanwhile, I had lost my job and had no clue what I was going to do next. I was unemployed for a longer period of time than I had ever anticipated. I was looking for another job and talking to a lot of my girlfriends who worked in the business. I sent resumes out for writers' assistant positions and anything else that I thought was going to bring me closer to the writers' room.

Finally, I got a call. I was blessed because I was able to tap into JaSheika's network. She had worked at ABC and ABC Studios for years, and through a couple of girlfriends over there, I heard about a pilot that was looking for a showrunner's assistant. The pilot was called *Bad Mom*. It starred Jenna Elfman and was written by *Catastrophe's* Sharon Horgan, who was already a star in Britain, but was just starting to break into the U.S. television market.

Sharon was working with two other comedy showrunners named Jennifer Crittenden and Gabrielle Allan. Jen and Gaby were looking for an assistant as they were getting ready to oversee Sharon's pilot as executive producers. I read the pilot and just like JaSheika with *Revenge*, I immediately thought, *"I have to work on this show."* It was right in line with the type of comedy that I love.

In hindsight, it was another moment I can look back on and say, *"There is a lot of power in the tongue."* When you say certain things, whether off-handedly or with conscious belief, you can manifest them. I ended up having a meeting with Gaby and Jen where I told them about my experience working with Yvette for years and the services I had provided as a showrunner's assistant. I told them how much I love comedy and how much I wanted to write but hadn't yet had the opportunity.

What clicked with them, and what I think cinched the job for me, was when I shared with them that I am a troubleshooter. If I don't know how to do something, I figure it out. That appealed to both Gaby and Jen because as showrunners, wives, and mothers, they did not have time to deal with minor administrative and logistical matters gone wrong—especially not during prep and production of a pilot when a trusty assistant could jump right in and take care of it all.

One of the things I learned in that first meeting was the value of knowing your worth when moving on to your next job. A lot of times we are so scared to ask for what we need and deserve as employees. When I applied to work with Gaby and Jen, I knew what I needed in order to survive—a lot more than the fee the studio allotted to showrunners for their assistants. But after six years working as a showrunner's assistant, I knew the value that I would bring to these two women as a highly experienced assistant. I made a decision to ask for what I was worth. Although it was scary and extremely uncomfortable—especially after not having worked for seven months—I knew that the worst thing that could happen was they'd say no, and we'd continue to negotiate. But they said *"yes,"* and as a result, today I know my worth, I know what I need, and I always ask for more.

Chapter Eleven

PEAKS AND VALLEYS

"Wait a second, wait a second, wait a second, there's a page missing out of my copy of the script."

— David Addison Jr., *Moonlighting*

JaSheika

For the first season of *Revenge*, I was a writers' assistant and the show became a colossal hit. During the second season, I was assigned my first script to co-write, thanks to Mike Kelley. In the third season of the show, I was staffed for the very first time. My dream of becoming a television writer was now my reality! I rejoiced, I celebrated, and had worked very hard for this position. But despite all of the years I'd prepared for this moment, I still feared I wasn't good enough.

Although I was finally on staff, I still had doubts about what I was capable of doing as a writer. Before, I had been afraid to admit what I wanted to do, but then after I had gotten over that fear and was finally writing, I constantly questioned whether I was good enough. I had the support of the room with my first script, but I still struggled with the expectations I placed on myself.

Every day I went into work petrified, questioning my ability. I was always in my head. I would sit in the room and write my pitches without speaking much. There's a lot of performance and salesmanship to pitching. Some people can get up and pitch a terrible story, but because of how they sell it, people would think it was amazing. I've always found that somewhat difficult because I'm terrible at performing and putting on a great show for a pitch. I'm all about being authentic.

One of the show's writers, an executive producer named Mark Perry, ended up giving me the best advice: *"Pitch without shame."* Don't ever worry if something is a good idea because the truth is, even if it's bad, it can spark something else that will bring out the best idea. That's what the whole process of breaking story in a writers' room is about—being collaborative and throwing ideas out there.

Revenge was a huge success for ABC Network. So successful, in fact, it became too big to fail. Mike eventually parted ways with the show and the network because of creative differences, and a new showrunner took over when I became a staff writer in the third season. When the season ended, I was called into the new showrunner's office and he began critiquing my performance for the season, saying that I didn't speak up enough, and when I did my pitches they didn't land, etc. etc. The conversation started to sound muddled in my ears as he continued, like the voice of the teacher from *Charlie Brown*. When he finished and asked if I had anything to say, all I could ask was why he hadn't given me that feedback earlier. He responded that he supposed he should have, but at the same time, I should have known. Given that I was a first-time staff writer, it was difficult for me to reconcile the fact that I *"should have known"* what I didn't know that I didn't know. You know? I wasn't a mind reader!

I was, however, my own worst critic, so him saying that was an affirmation of my own fears that I wasn't good enough. I internalized that belief, and it sent me into a dark depression. *If this is what this business is about, I don't want to be a part of it,* I thought. For the entire season, I didn't know that I was doing anything wrong. I was always criticizing myself, but when somebody else said it, I felt like people hadn't been truthful with me all along.

I didn't get the option renewed on my contract after that. (An "option" is a choice a showrunner can make to exercise, or not, when it comes to renewing your contract as a writer for a show's next season.) Not getting an option picked up in the writer's world is like getting fired. I felt like I was a failure. *Here I am, someone who has talked about this dream for years, I finally get it, and then I fail,* I thought. I started to think that my dream was not meant to be.

I wanted to turn away from writing for TV altogether. I was so ashamed and embarrassed. My sister was the only one who knew that my option was not picked up. I didn't even talk to my agent about it. My agent was my representative at the time who helped negotiate my contract with the showrunner and studio. They are the representative of writers who pitch you to meet with various studio and network executives, producers, and showrunners. So, not discussing what happened on the job with my agent and giving him my perspective put me at a great disadvantage.

Over the next month, I scrutinized every action I took during that season and asked myself what I could have done better. The experience was soul-crushing, but I kept my pain on the inside. Now that I'm older, I know better. One of the things that we have learned is when in doubt, focus out. And also, speak it out. It's not good to carry the burden of doubt or embarrassment or sadness alone. Share it with your peers, with your family, or a therapist, if necessary, so that you don't have to take it all on by yourself. Carrying it alone impacts you physically, emotionally, and even creatively to a certain degree. If you don't have the strength to fight against negative thoughts and beliefs by yourself, then somebody else can help you kickstart it.

There's a joke in the TV writing community that you're not truly a writer until you've been fired. That's because everybody's been fired from a job or let go unexpectedly, or a job has ended early. The first hurdle for me was realizing that not having my option picked up, or being let go, is not the end of the world and it's definitely not the end of a career.

I had already scheduled a vacation to Greece with a group of girlfriends for after the show's season ended. I decided to still go, even though I felt like I was escaping reality by doing so. While I was on vacation, I was told that my agent had a conversation with my former showrunner and something about me being "lazy" came up. It horrified me. I've always prided myself on having a strong work ethic. The fact that that word was used to describe me to my rep, whose job it is to support and pitch me to other executives and showrunners for potential jobs, was a huge blow.

But timing is everything. While in Greece in the summer of 2014, I met my future husband, Francesko. And if I wasn't in the headspace I was in, I don't know if I would have been open to allowing somebody into my life. One fateful night on the island of Mykonos, my girlfriends and I walked into a popular bar lounge called Semeli. Five or ten minutes later, my now husband walked in and it was love at first sight. It was as if our souls had known each other for years. He laid eyes on me the previous night and when he saw me for a second time, he made sure not to miss his chance to introduce himself. He chatted me up, offered me a drink, we danced the night away, and the rest is history.

Meeting my husband was a healing moment that came at a time when I was debating, *"Which road am I going to take? Am I going to get off this pathway?"* I was seriously considering giving up my dream, all because of that one bad experience. Being from a different country and not knowing my line of work, Francesko's responses to what I was going through were very practical. I could have all these complicated thoughts in my head and then when I'd share them with him, he'd offer clear and straightforward solutions. *"How did I not think of that?"* I'd say. He reminded me that the showrunner who critiqued my work as a writer was *"just one guy."* I could get another job and somebody else would love me, my writing, and what I bring to a room. My logical head should already have known that, but with the simplicity of his words, he was able to knock me out of the fog I was in and help me believe in myself again.

JaNeika

You know the saying, *"Beauty is in the eye of the beholder"*? Well, the same goes for success. Success is defined in different ways to different people. After I was hired to work on *Bad Mom* for the salary I desired, some may have looked at my experience from the outside and called me "successful." The assumption is, now that you're moving in your purpose for what you're worth, everything is going to be smooth and easy. Unfortunately, "success" doesn't mean your problems go away. Instead, you start learning how to solve different problems.

I remember listening to Jasmine Guy (who played Whitley Gilbert in *A Different World*) as the keynote speaker at the Image Initiative's *Sisters Empowering Sisters Conference* in Syracuse, New York. In her speech, she spoke of how people would come up to her and mention her marriage as a great accomplishment because of how long she was married, and she thought: *"But I don't really even know my husband; I'm still getting to know that man every day. I'm still learning myself every single day."*

I feel like the same can be said about our profession. We're learning new things about ourselves, and our jobs as creatives, every single day. It's not like we become successful and then all of a sudden, our issues, doubts, and fears suddenly disappear. We continue to grow, evolve, and get stronger while pushing past them.

We're the only ones who get to determine our own capabilities.

We don't have to internalize other people's limited ideas and interpretations of what our capabilities are. As dream pursuers and manifestors, we're the only ones who get to determine our own capabilities. While those who are in leadership positions at any given corporation, institution, or job hold the keys to positions and opportunities that may get us one step closer to our dreams and goals, they don't ultimately control our destinies.

As JaSheika was navigating the unexpected turns in her career, I was questioning what was happening for me. JaSheika had transitioned to a network television show as a writer's assistant and then quickly became a writer on *Revenge* without me. We were writing partners; we had been introduced around town as a writing team, but she ended up getting a job that did not include me. That was difficult for me to digest initially because I had been the one working directly under showrunners who could hire me for their writing staffs, should they have their shows picked up. It was exciting to see JaSheika finally get her seat at the table, but I was feeling a little sad for myself.

After two years, my job with Gaby and Jen ended and I found myself, once again, unemployed. They were able to help me get another job working for Sharon Horgan, the star and creator of *Bad Mom*, who had another pilot greenlit by ABC, called *Bad Management.* That took the sting out of my stint with Gaby and Jen coming to an end because it meant I was only unemployed for three months this time, instead of seven. One of the things that helped me throughout the transitional period when JaSheika was hired as a writer and I was not, was something our agent, Howie Tanenbaum at ICM, said.

He told us, *"You know what? This job, this career, this journey, this pursuit of this dream, it's a marathon, it's not a sprint. Right now, JaSheika's being hired and we're going to celebrate that because it's a huge accomplishment. At a certain point, we're going to come back around to the two of you being together, but just keep in mind, we're in this for the long haul, so think of it as a marathon."* At the time, I remember thinking, *"Okay, cool, but I have been working under showrunners for eight years and I'm still not staffed! But great, Howie."*

Over time, however, Howie's advice became something that helped me think about my strategies moving forward. It helped me look at myself and the choices I was making and consider how I could get to where I wanted to be, in a different way. Usually when you're dating a few people consecutively and none of the relationships progress toward your intended outcome, you take a look at the common factor (usually yourself) and make adjustments. In my case, the common factor was comedy. Once I realized that, my agent Howie would eventually come through on his promise of bringing me and JaSheika back together in the marathon.

Chapter Twelve

GAINING MOMENTUM

"Did I do that?"

— Steve Urkel, *Family Matters*

JaNeika

With all of the various changes going on with our careers at the time, one of the things that helped us throughout our highs and lows was acquiring a new perspective. We shifted not only the way we saw ourselves and our goals, but also the world.

After my jobs subsequently ended with all of the phenomenal female comedy showrunners I worked with—from Yvette to Jen, Gaby, and Sharon—I thought to myself, *something's got to give. Something's got to change. I've been working for comedy showrunners for eight years and yet, here I am... still not staffed!* My sister went from working at a major studio in post-production to a one-hour show and was staffed within a year. That's when it suddenly occurred to me: *I should probably think about getting some one-hour experience.* So, that became my new goal. As we mentioned earlier, dreams sometimes shift; I wanted to diversify my resume.

One of the reasons we enjoyed the idea of being comedy writers is because we'd get roughly the same amount of money for fewer pages to write. I was thinking that was going to be a shortcut. One of the things I quickly learned about myself is that while I was really funny on the page, being funny in the room was a very different story.

Comedy rooms are some of the best rooms to work in when they're run efficiently by humans who happen to have a conscience and understand the plight of other human beings. The ones I have worked in have always made me feel as if I was going to work to play every day, which is fun because most comedy writers spend their days cracking jokes with each other to see which ones stick to the board for story. We could spend hours in the best comedy rooms being entertained all day by comedians who have a sixth sense for joke-telling. It's organically unstoppable for most.

I remember the first time I met stand-up comedian, Sinbad, when I interviewed Eileen Mack Knight for my master's thesis. Upon meeting him, it was joke after joke after joke for the entire five minutes he was in the office before he left. Comedians and comedic writers have a natural desire to make people laugh. There's great satisfaction in it, which is beautiful but also terrifying for somebody who doesn't naturally have that innate skill.

So, while I was having a good time being funny on the page writing comedy spec scripts and pilots, it did not seem to be in the cards for me to get staffed in a comedy writing room. I thought it was probably why I had worked for so long in comedy, yet had not gotten staffed. It wasn't meant to be... yet!

So, I started to apply for jobs with one-hour shows and I ended up getting a job working for a woman named Maggie Malina. She was the non-writing executive producer for a VH1 series called *Hit the Floor*. She had worked at MTV Networks and VH1 for years before she got a producing deal and was able to shepherd the VH1 network into scripted programming with shows and TV movies including *Single Ladies, CrazySexyCool: The TLC Story,* and *Hindsight.*

Maggie was a creative producer but not a writer. When I started working for her, she had one foot in the door as a VH1 executive, but she was also on the creative side in production as executive producer on *Hit the Floor*. Working in one-hour television at VH1 was an eye-opening experience on many levels. *Hit the Floor* was my first foray into drama production on an on-going series. I was able to witness and learn the ins and outs of what it takes to produce a drama from concept to screen. It was also the first time I worked on a show that was intricately informed by the music it featured. Because VH1 was formerly a music video channel, working on its scripted series and films was a dream come true as it blended two of my favorite loves—music and television. Through my position working with Maggie, I gained a new perspective on working in the industry. Before this, I had always worked for the sellers—the showrunners, the writers—people who were trying to pitch and sell TV shows to executives.

Because of Maggie's very unique position, I was able to get the perspective of being on the buyer's side, which I had never seen. To reiterate: to achieve dreams, it's important to open your mind and visualize what certain situations may look like. In the same way that visiting the set at *Dawson's Creek* helped us envision ourselves in that space, having access to the buyer's side of the industry gave me my first true view into what it looks like to sell yourself as a writer.

When I was with Yvette, Gaby, and Jen, I helped with their development, typing pitch cards and putting their decks together. But I never got to go out and watch them do the pitching. Being at Maggie's desk, I was able to read scripts, give feedback, and help prepare for her meetings, but then I got to watch people come in, present themselves, and try to sell their ideas. In doing so, the mystique around what it takes to pitch and sell a show was removed. All this time, I had been holding the idea of being a writer as something so far removed from me— way up high, above me somewhere. The reality was that the writers themselves, and becoming a writer, was not far from me at all.

After reading various documents and watching people come in and pitch, I thought to myself, *I can do this.* Then, I'd read some of the scripts and the pilots that were submitted and think, *I can write circles around these people! Why am I holding myself so small when it comes to my dream?* I should have seen myself as being amongst the people who had already achieved the dream. That simple shift in perspective completely changed the way I operated. Because I started to envision myself in these positions, doors began to open so that I no longer held myself so far away from them.

While working for Maggie, I'd gone into my ninth year in the industry. It was in 2005 that JaSheika and I were living in Burbank and declared that if we didn't get staffed in ten years, we were out of there. The pressure of coming up to that ten-year point made me want to do some self-reflection. So, I took part in an experiential training program and did just that.

Similar to how JaSheika's husband, Francesko, shifted her perspective by simplifying what had seemed so complicated in her head, I also started to shift my perspective.

Everything that I held so tight and narrow when it came to my career, getting staffed, and becoming a writer, I started to release. I balanced my life out a little bit more. I got involved in community service. I started exercising and prioritizing self-care and wellness. I started to date, which was a miracle in itself given my perspective on dating, years prior, when I first moved to Los Angeles.

I had been so focused on getting staffed as a writer for years, I felt I didn't have time to be social or to consider my personal life. I remember at one point telling Yvette that the idea of getting staffed on my first show turned me on more than the idea of hopping on the internet to find a dude to date. And there went my twenties—in pursuit of happiness... writing. But it's when I started to balance out various sectors of my life emotionally, physically, spiritually, romantically, and service-wise that things started to shift. It's almost as if holding on so tightly to a dream doesn't allow the dream to flow.

After reading various documents and watching people come in and pitch, I thought to myself, I can do this.

The irony is that we got so deeply in pursuit of this dream that brought us joy, that we lost sight of the joy amid the pursuit.

So, my advice to anyone reading who is feeling a little stuck or blocked from what your life's purpose is: Do something to address it now, while you can. Whether it's therapy, life coaching, or some form of personal development where you can gain tools to look inside and see how you can better yourself in order to move forward, go for it! Opening my eyes and my life to the possibility of all that it could actually entail is what made the difference for me. It's so important to cultivate the fullness of the dream life you deserve because it allows everything that you want to flow into your life that much faster.

***

While I was working for Maggie, I saw an opportunity to apply to a writing-intensive program through FOX. The entertainment industry holds a number of annual programs to help develop writers in TV and film. They are put in place to serve underrepresented communities such as people of color, women, LGBTQ+, etc. There was something about FOX's program that appealed to me. It was for people who had a little bit of success in the business or who had already worked in it for a long time, but hadn't been able to get over that hump to kickstart their careers. That was me. I'd had a vast amount of experience working for some truly incredible women in television, but I still had not had the opportunity to show what I could do in terms of writing.

To apply to the FOX Writing Intensive program, I needed a recommendation from a rep, a showrunner, or an executive to even get the application. I emailed my sister's agent Howie, and said, *"I'm trying to get into this program. Do you mind referring me?"* He didn't mind, so he hip-pocketed me to get an application. Hip-pocketing meant he wouldn't officially be working for me, but he could do some business on my behalf.

What I did not know was that Howie reached out to Gina Reyes, the head of the FOX Writing Intensive program at the time, and asked for an application for a writing team. When I requested the application for FOX, I was operating as an individual writer; I wrote by myself. But Howie, with his foresight, still saw JaSheika and me as a writing team, so he asked for an application for both of us. JaSheika and I figured, *why don't we just apply together?* So, we did, and we got an interview for the program, but we did not get selected. This was another example of how God always prepares us for things. Remember when JaSheika wasn't initially chosen for the ABC Associates Program? This time around wasn't so bad. Especially when we were chosen as alternates—part of the top ten applicants.

We were videotaped talking to a camera during the interview process. That video was then sent out to executives throughout 20th Century FOX Studios and the FOX Network who would determine who should become a part of their brand. Being in front of cameras is the antithesis of what writers are about; we're not actors. We don't perform. So, the whole time, JaSheika and I were incredibly uncomfortable.

But one of the things I appreciate and respect about the FOX program is that once you are accepted, you're in it for life. It allows you to build a relationship with the studio in a way that fosters your talent and progression as a writer. They invest in you, your growth, and your promotion, whereas in other programs, you can be used as a "diversity hire" for a year because a studio offers to pay for your inclusion. Once that year is over, however, the obligation to your program contract is completed and you may never work in a writer's room again.

The FOX program's goal was to bring underrepresented communities into writer's rooms and continue to foster that talent from writer to story editor to executive story editor, and so on should the show fit. Even if the TV show you were working on was canceled, they would try to make sure another FOX TV show kept you in the fold. It was refreshing and encouraging.

So, we were alternates, which was a little shocking because I thought we crushed the interview. But as it turned out, two weeks into the program, we were invited to join. Again, JaSheika's experience with the ABC Production Associates program had already prepared us for this.

We became part of the FOX Writing Intensive class of 2015. We were one step closer to the dream of being staffed. For anyone constantly being told *"No"* and having recurring thoughts of not being good enough—stop it NOW! We're all good enough. And sometimes... rejection is God's protection. *"No"* could just mean *"not right now."*

JaSheika

After not having my option picked up on *Revenge*, I went through a phase of questioning whether I was going to stick with this career. I went to Greece, had a great vacation, met my future husband, came back, but then had a dormant period. I wrote one of my great friends and mentors, Wendy Calhoun, who had also worked on *Revenge* during the first season. She wrote back and told me to call her immediately.

I called Wendy and shared my story about what happened. She gave me some great advice and said, *"There are so many people in your position with your background who don't know what they're going to do next. This happens all the time."* It was refreshing to hear because there I was thinking it was the end of the world. I had my opportunity, and I'd blown it. But Wendy explained, *"No! This was normal and a part of being in the business."* She continued, *"I know people who were in the position you're in who had to take a step back in order to move forward."*

Wendy then told me about this show she was recently staffed on. It was co-created by Lee Daniels and Danny Strong, called *Empire*. *"Have you heard about it?"* she asked. I told her I knew about it because I'd read the script. The pilot was so bold and brash, I thought there was no way it was going to get picked up by network TV.

She told me to send her my resume. I thought, *Maybe I can get staffed!* Unfortunately, that was not the case. They were already staffed with writers, but they were looking to hire support staff—writers' assistants or script coordinators.

I had a moment where my ego stood out front and center. *What are people going to think?* I wondered. *I was a staff writer and now I have to take a step back?* I sent my resume anyway and went in for an interview with Ilene Chaiken, the showrunner at the time. I told her about my previous experience being staffed, and she asked, *"How do you feel?"* She meant, in regard to me considering a position that was, indeed, a step backward. I told her, *"I'm just looking for an opportunity. I would love to be in a room among writers again."*

I took the job as script coordinator in Season One. I had come off a show where I was told I was *"lazy,"* which was a mischaracterization of my character. Still, I made sure I busted my ass when I got the job on *Empire*. I worked above and beyond what was required of me. *Nobody's ever going to question whether I'm a hard worker again*, I thought. Of course, it paid off.

Part Four

LOOK AT US NOW

Climax: *An action the character takes out of the crisis. (The point of no return. This is the height of the story. It will turn for better or worse for our hero.)*

Chapter Thirteen

A SEAT AT THE TABLE

*"I want a seat at the adults' table like I was during the election.
Or have you forgotten how things worked back then?"*

— Mellie Fitzgerald, *Scandal*

JaSheika

Even though I didn't have the title, I had the opportunity to be in the writers' room when I started on the new show, *Empire*. As a script coordinator, I continued to hone my writing craft, all while working hard to make an impression. I impressed the showrunner to the extent that, when my sister and I did get the opportunity to be part of the FOX Writing Intensive program, it was a no-brainer for Ilene to want JaNeika and me to come on as writers for the second season of the show. *Full-time* writers. Thanks to our agent, the FOX Writing Intensive program, and all those years of manifesting our dream of becoming television writers, we were finally able to have a seat at the table, together.

Climax is an action a character takes out of the crisis they've experienced. It is the point of no return. Working at *Empire* was our climax moment.

I took a step back to work as the script coordinator and in hindsight, it was probably the best decision I ever made. I got to see what it was like to create in an unconventional writers' room. Whereas normal writers' rooms consist of writers who have either been staffed previously on other shows or have some sort of experience in TV, this room was different because it was created by Lee Daniels and Danny Strong, two successful filmmakers who had yet to produce their own TV series. This was their first foray into creating for network television.

It was fascinating, to say the least. They got Ilene Chaiken, the creator of *The L Word,* to come and run this show about an African-American family in the music business. It was so unconventional because there were some people with experience in TV, like my friend Wendy Calhoun, and then there were others who came from film, and still others who were former music video directors, playwrights, and even novelists.

Everything Lee did up to that point was unconventional. As an independent filmmaker, he would raise money to produce his films outside the studio system. The stories he told were not necessarily mainstream. Having such a diverse group of people who were so far off from what was considered the Hollywood norm contributed to why *Empire* became such a huge success. Typically, writers' rooms would have maybe one or two people of color—if you're lucky. In its first season, the *Empire* writers' room was a diverse room, with the majority people of color.

Since it was Lee's first foray into television, the first three weeks he came into the room very excited. He shared all these wild, crazy experiences he'd had in an effort to help shape the scope of the characters he and Danny created with a sense of truth and authenticity that could only come from his real life. The writers also shared stories and life experiences that helped fuel the drive of the characters, and shaped the stories that were told in the first season.

One of the greatest things about the show, in Season One, was that it was created in a vacuum. The creators, showrunner, and writers didn't have any clue how audiences across the world would respond to *Empire* once it aired. And when it did, most—if not all—of the scripts were written, and episodes were shot. There is freedom and joy one experiences when they're able to create without consideration. Most of the hit shows I've worked on became phenomena as a result of such freedom.

In any industry, one of the most important things a leader can do is connect to people as human beings. That is key to any type of success. It's also what brings joy to the job. When we lose sight of experiencing joy, we lose sight of ourselves and why we do what we do. That's not the type of success I ever aspire to have.

During Season One of *Empire*, many music industry veterans visited the writers' room and shared their experiences to help ensure the show was as authentic in its storytelling as possible. We had Timbaland's wife, Monique Idlett-Mosley, Gladys Knight, and Rick Rubin to name a few. It was exciting. We had way too much fun creating extreme, outlandish, and unexpected storylines, but there were also moments that encompassed heartfelt truth.

I remember Lee asking me, *"What do you think? Do you think this show's going to last?"* He and Danny were operating from a place of, *"Well, hell, if this don't last, we're going to throw in everything and the kitchen sink because we don't know how long this is going to go for."* I told him, *"I've worked on hit shows before and my gut is telling me that you're good. It's going to be okay."* He said, *"Okay, I'm going to listen to you, little girl."*

I was so Zen before the show premiered—it was the same sense of calm that came over me before *Revenge* premiered. When it did, the ratings (the number of viewers it had) were exceptional and had everyone talking. FOX did a massive, beautiful marketing campaign promoting its new, musical drama starring Terrence Howard and Taraji P. Henson. When the show aired in its second week, to everyone's surprise... the ratings rose! In the third week, the ratings rose again.

One of the most important things a leader can do is connect to people as human beings.

Every week *Empire* aired during Season One, the ratings went up, up, and up. It was a cultural phenomenon.

Empire attracted the coveted demographic advertisers care about, which is the group of viewers who are between the ages of eighteen and thirty-four. The ratings went from a 3.8 for the pilot to a 6.9 by the final episode in Live+ Same Day viewership. It was talked about on the news every single week because its meteoric rise was unprecedented, unlike anything anyone had ever seen before.

It was like the little show that could. It had the media behind it because of people like Terrence and Taraji, but it also brought fresh talent from actors Jussie Smollett, Trai Byers, and Bryshere "Yazz" Gray onto the world stage.

I truly believe that because of the creators' commitment to not following "the rules" as predicated by other people, the show became a huge success. Lee and Danny came with their own set of rules, which was to have fun. They didn't care about what they were "supposed" to do, which is why that first season is so high impact and high octane. Something crazy happened every episode because they were like, *"You know what? We only got one shot. This is our chance to take it."*

They didn't follow conventional storytelling and structure. In Hollywood, the traditional drama has a few main characters and an A, B, and C story to follow. We had five main characters we were telling stories for, along with musical stories and performances. A lot of what *Empire* did was unconventional— starting with the lead characters consisting of an African-American family, which was something that had not been seen in a really long time, particularly in American television drama.

There were a lot of predominantly Black television shows on the air in the 1990s and then all of a sudden, there was a complete lack of them. Not only did this drop affect representation on-screen, but also behind the scenes. There were a lot of African-American creatives, once thriving in the '90s and early 2000s, who hadn't worked in years. Their careers were at a standstill.

What *Empire* did was revive interest in stories about people of color in an unabashed, unapologetic way. It told stories about rich Black people, which audiences had rarely seen on network television. It was an all-Black cast for a one-hour drama, before *Insecure, Atlanta, Greenleaf,* and *Queen Sugar.* Now, we have this emergence of Black television and Black representation all over again.

There are a lot of African-American writers talking about how we are in a golden age, but it can go away, all of a sudden, all over again. The decline in African-American shows being produced in the late '90s just happened; it's a weird cycle. Black programming is niche programming; Black and Latino audiences are generally used to establish a foundation for a network, but then once the network starts to take off, or "crossover" with what's considered a mainstream hit ("mainstream" sometimes equates to white or broader audiences), then the networks tend to turn their backs on the loyal initial audiences that helped them get their start. But that's show business; it looks to broaden the audience and broaden income potential.

The revelation with *Empire* is that, with those numbers, it wasn't just Black and Brown audiences tuning in each week. The biggest audience for *Empire* in the first season was white women over forty. So, that whole myth that you can't do anything that is predominantly African-American or of color and have it cross over or be mainstream was busted wide open by the fact that the ratings kept rising. The show had twenty-two million viewers for the first season finale.

There was a local spot in the valley called the Man Cave that would have watch parties and air the show live for fans. During the series finale, the place was so packed it was standing room only with a line outside waiting to enter. Witnessing this huge reception was incredible. Every week, we'd watch the show live with east and west coast audiences and live tweet with the fans. I felt so proud to be a part of a groundbreaking show that sparked gatherings and watch parties across the nation.

What this business can use is the elimination of limiting ideas about how we connect as human beings outside of our cultural distinctions, our sexual identities, and our politics. For the most part, I feel that we connect as human beings on a much broader scale, and *Empire* was at the forefront of that.

As a minority working in this business, we're told there is not a lot of interest in these stories because they don't increase the studios' profits from international sales. Every studio looks to make bank off of their products domestically, but also in other countries. They're thinking about making as much money as they possibly can, so we're often hit with this idea that our stories are not as universal as other stories, or as valuable. The cool thing about the times we live in now is that the world is proving that this belief is unequivocally untrue. It's a myth, not a fact. One of my and JaNeika's goals is to eradicate this false theory out of the minds of leaders in our industry through our work, advocacy, and storytelling.

Chapter Fourteen

CURATING GREAT NETWORKS

"Ladies, don't ever let what a man brings to the table be all you have to eat."

— Clair Huxtable, *The Cosby Show*

JaSheika

The TV business is not for the weary. We took our time to get where we wanted to go. One of the things I admire about millennials is they're not willing to wait forever to achieve their goals. A lot of people complain about that, but I respect it; if I had that gumption and can-do attitude, I probably wouldn't have taken ten years to get to where I am. I probably would have said I'd get there in two years, and that would have come true. But I have an appreciation for the time that it took us because it allowed us to build character.

If we jumped from working as assistants to being showrunners, I'm not sure that we would understand or respect any of the positions that work under us in the way that they deserve, because we would've missed the journey that those positions provide. I don't know that in two years we would have been ready to be where we are now. We wouldn't have had the scope of understanding that we have of what goes into writing, producing, and delivering a show.

Because it took us so long and because we worked in different areas of television, we are better leaders. We try to help and support the assistants who work on our shows now. We're always trying to come to their defense and encourage them while they're in their current positions—whether they're working in the art department, on set as ADs, in props, or costumes or casting. Instead of being short-tempered and frustrated when something is going wrong or we're not able to get the things that we need from them in the moment, we have compassion and empathy because we've been in those positions. We understand that they're doing the best that they can.

In any industry, there are career peaks and valleys. As somebody who had dreams and ambitions of becoming a writer, I had been so excited to get into a writers' room. And for the most part, throughout the first seasons of hit shows I worked on, my experiences were great. I would think, *"I can't believe this is my job!"* But what I noticed with hit shows is that there are times where things take a turn—usually in the second season. I don't know if it's a result of success or a combination of egos and personality clashes, but there's something that creates a stain in the process.

I think a lot of those problems are a result of people's own insecurities. There were times when JaNeika and I would take certain comments personally and we'd leave the room feeling like we weren't good enough, or that our contribution didn't matter. It was so exciting to finally be at the table, but then when we didn't feel acknowledged or valued and the things that we were bringing forth were consistently being dismissed, it was difficult to continue to get joy from the position we were in.

JaNeika

As staff writers, one of the things we learned was that our voices weren't heard as loudly as those of the upper-level staff. Sometimes we'd pitch ideas that were either not well-received or received at all. Then a few minutes later an upper-level writer would pitch what essentially felt like the same thing, but instead would receive great reception to what we had just said moments prior. That is a normal part of the staff writer experience on a TV show. You are seen, but not necessarily heard all the time. While it is normal, it's not something JaSheika and I ever really got used to.

As creative people, our creative nature must be nurtured. Erykah Badu coined it perfectly when she famously sang, *"I'm an artist and I'm sensitive about my shit."* We are so very sensitive as creatives, because we're passionate about our works of art—in our case, our writing. Like any other artist who takes part in this business, we seek validation of our creative expression due to the depths of vulnerability we must reach to get to a place where we feel comfortable openly expressing ourselves through our works. A lot is unearthed in our writing, and when there is no acknowledgment of it, at best, we carry on without any form of validation in our works, good or bad. At worst, we internalize it and it affects our performance. It affects our ability to be creative. It affects our ability to continue to thrive within our dream.

One of the things that we recognized very early on in our careers is how important it is to connect with people on a human level, and not just strictly on a business level for professional benefits. We're not on this journey called life alone, and we're also not trying to succeed in this business alone.

Years later, we put together a creative collective of friends and peers, so that people who experienced some of the same feelings and emotions and even had some of the same questions we did earlier in our careers, could come together and be acknowledged in knowing: We are not alone in our journeys. We believe, *"My success does not have to equal your loss."* It is possible to create a world where everyone can win. JaSheika and I prefer to look at life that way, instead of the alternative.

We're not on this journey called life alone, and we're also not trying to succeed in this business alone.

JaSheika

After my experience of getting on a show, getting staffed, and then not getting my option picked up and having to revive my career, I thought, *how many other people have experienced what I experienced, and don't know how to get back up?* I got the idea to start a support group, which I called Creative Artists Connect (CAC). The purpose of it was to bring creatives together—writers, producers, directors, actors, whomever—who were up-and-coming in the business.

If there are people in a room treating others poorly, it's because they have been treated poorly in the past, too. Hurt people hurt people, but we don't have to take those experiences and do the same in return. We can break the cycle. The tendency in Hollywood is to be in competition with others or to step on people or push them down to get them to work harder and better. But people work better when they are supported and enjoying their job. People need to feel good in order to thrive in this business. Through CAC, I wanted to make sure other people coming up in the business knew that they had the power to create positive change.

Some people would say the group was *"like therapy."* So many were going through such similar things. CAC was a place where they could share those experiences, but also offer support and help others shift their perspectives. We would give examples of actions they could take to stand in their strength and be empowered to use their voices. We work in a business where we are encouraged to share our creativity and express ourselves, but if it's not in line with how some people feel we should express ourselves, then they want to silence us, which is the worst thing someone can do to a creative person. It's like trying to muzzle a lion; it will hurt the animal just as much as it hurts you!

If you're a creative professional and you can't find your tribe or group, you can create your own and recognize the power that you have to shift and influence the world. It's a very bold intention to think that you can change a whole culture in an industry that has made a lot of money off the backs of others, but change has to start from somewhere. The Civil Rights and Women's Rights movements began because people had the courage to recognize their power and continued to move forward despite their fears.

Mahatma Gandhi is known for his famous quote, *"Be the change that you want to see."* The "Me Too" and the "Black Lives Matter" movements have shown that the status quo in the entertainment industry can no longer prevail when it is to the detriment of marginalized groups. As future leaders in the industry, we want to impart that we can create a group in unison that declares, *"We don't get down with the status quo."*

Chapter Fifteen

EQUAL PLAYING FIELD – WORK/LIFE BALANCE

"Could we speed this up please? We have families at home waiting for us."

— Mary Jenkins, *227*

JaNeika

For so long, I thought, *"To achieve the dream, you have to be focused on the dream."* And narrowly focused on it, I was. As I mentioned earlier, there were times when I was so closed off to other opportunities and experiences throughout my twenties because I was determined to get staffed as a writer. Something that is crucial for writers, or any other creatives serious about their craft, is life experience.

I wanted to get to a place where I earned enough to "deserve" a vacation, or a trip to the movies, or dinner with friends. I even denied myself the self-care needed to feel good about myself—like going to the gym, volunteering, or going to church. By limiting my life experience primarily to work, I cut myself off to the creative and energetic flow that would allow me to achieve my dream at an even greater capacity.

It wasn't until I put attention and energy into different areas of my life outside of work that my dream of becoming a writer started to come true. When I committed to a decision to focus on dating, prioritize my nutrition and health, and make time for church, it was almost three months before the ten-year deadline I gave myself. That's when things started to fall in place. I started earning more money and I was accepted into FOX's Writing Intensive program. I started going out, spending more time with friends, and enjoying life. Almost to the day of the ten-year mark, I received a call informing me that I was going to be staffed as a writer on *Empire*.

I came to realize the power in declaring what it is that you want, when you want it. I learned not to cut myself off from important life experiences in order to achieve what I deemed the ultimate experience. Self-care, wellness, venturing out and meeting new people, and touching base within social circles are just a few of the experiences needed to achieve the dream. They're all a part of living, and to create at the highest levels, we have to live. Otherwise, what stories do we have to tell?

JaSheika

My experience is similar to JaNeika's in the sense that things started to shift when I allowed someone special to come into my life. Often, I say that my husband saved me. I say this mainly because he has a completely different perspective on life, so when I told him about the things that were troubling me in mine, he helped me shift my perspective. If I said, *"They said this about me,"* he would say, *"But it's not true, so why does it matter what they said?"* It's a simple shift, but when he said it, I finally heard it.

Work/life balance is something I'm still working on right now. My husband comes from a country where the women stay at home; they cook, they clean, and they raise the children while the men go out and work. I am an ambitious career woman, and I still have more that I want to accomplish. Not to say that I don't clean, but I don't clean. I pay somebody to come clean for me. I cook, but only when I have time. I don't have children yet, so there's a strong chance I'll succeed in that area. I am a work in progress, in that regard.

Right now, I'm working on getting pregnant. It's crazy when I think about it because we're probably going to be running a show and shooting a pilot, and

I'll be very busy. But at the same time, I get excited about the fact that I'll get to bring my kid with me to enjoy all those experiences! I look forward to having my babies in the writers' room, on set, seeing the magic behind the screen, and witnessing their mommy be a boss—just like I watched my mom work at her various jobs when I was growing up.

JaNeika

The beauty is, we each get to create and define our own experiences. JaSheika is already dispelling the myth of what being married and successful looks like. She's not at home taking care of kids and cooking while her man goes out to work. She works just as hard as him to ensure their household secures all of the additional dreams they're seeking to achieve together. We get to cultivate what our family lives look like, the same way we get to curate and cultivate our dreams.

Although at times they can be useful, to a degree, life involves throwing plans and preparation out the door. Life doesn't have to look the way society expects it to; it's going to look how we create it to look. Take love and romance, for example. I don't say that I'm looking for love; I'm looking to create the space for the kind of love I want to find me.

I'd be lying if I said I didn't have fears around not finding love and being able to have the family I hope to create one day. Despite that fear, I continue to envision what having divine, authentic love with my husband and children is going to look like for me, and how amazing it's going to feel when I finally have it. Regardless of what others' expectations are in terms of when marriage and children will become a part of my life, I have my own destiny that is on no one else's timetable.

One practice JaSheika and I haven't often been great at is taking moments to be in gratitude for all we've accomplished. We've always been so caught up in the doing, that we rarely take moments to reflect on the being.

A good friend of ours, Kristen Carter, has a great habit of celebrating her accomplishments on social media. She expresses gratitude and truly savors her moments of achievement. I truly admire it, because JaSheika and I had never really taken the time to give ourselves the acknowledgment we want and deserve. This speaks to what I mentioned earlier, about creatives and our desire to be acknowledged and validated. If I don't look at myself in the mirror and say, *"Hey, girl, you did that. You're amazing! You just got staffed for the first time after working so hard for ten years,"* how can I expect it from other people? It's important to practice patting ourselves on the back and not feeling guilty about it.

Practicing gratitude not only creates what we can expect in return, but it also serves as a reminder of how far we've come. JaSheika and I were these two little latchkey kids, babysat by television in Germany, who then grew up in the racially-divided deep South. Since then, we've been featured in *Essence* magazine, *The Hollywood Reporter*, and *Variety*. We've been able to share our story and achievement in hopes of inspiring others to pursue their own uncharted dreams.

Looking back on the awards I received in middle school for the National Junior Honor Society, or getting a high school diploma, and graduating from college, even getting a master's degree; I realize those were all achievements I could have acknowledged better. If we start the practice of savoring moments of celebration at a very early age, they serve as proof down the road of what we've already accomplished. Once we've achieved something in the past, it becomes crystal clear—we have the ability to do it again.

We are always looking at how much further we have to go, but we need to remember to look back at where we started and celebrate how far we've come.

JaSheika

It's also important to acknowledge where we are. We are always looking at how much further we have to go, but we need to remember to look back at where we started and celebrate how far we've come. So often we beat ourselves up for not yet reaching our goals and being where we strive to be. The truth is, as long as we are taking the steps to get closer to our dreams, we should look to celebrate the journey along the way. When we arrive where we want to be, it's not only the achievement that makes us proud. It's also the commitment, the effort, and sacrifices it took to get us there. Too often we lose sight of the power in reflecting on the journey.

Part Five

REFLECTIONS OF TWO TV ADDICTS TURNED TV CREATORS

Resolution: *How the main character's life has changed (or not) as a result of the journey she's taken.*

Chapter Sixteen

IMPOSSIBLE = I'M POSSIBLE

"Impossible things are happening everyday"
— Fairy Godmother, ABC's Rodgers & Hammerstein's *Cinderella*

JaNeika

Wanting to be a TV writer for so long, then having my first writing job be on one of the biggest shows to premiere in 2015, made things that I never dreamed possible, suddenly possible. It is an incredible moment in my professional history, of which I will forever be grateful. But, as with any dream that finally comes to fruition, another reality comes right along with it.

While I was on this high of having my first job as a writer, I discovered that at staff level, I was required to contribute in ways that support upper-level writers in the room, in addition to the showrunner's vision of the show. We were not head writers; we could have a very clear idea of what we wanted to write in an episode, but that didn't necessarily mean our ideas were in line with what the showrunner preferred in the final version of the script.

I remember being so proud of the first draft of episode 205 of *Empire* that JaSheika and I wrote, along with our co-writer, Wendy Calhoun. Andre Lyon was getting baptized at church, which was a big deal for the show. It was an experience that JaSheika and I had the summer between fourth and fifth grades when we visited our grandparents in Detroit, Michigan. So, to bring a baptism to light and have it as a part of one of our main character's journey was exciting for us.

But there were things I did not take into consideration when it came to writing our first script. While we were excited about the baptism storyline, what we wrote was not aligned with the showrunner's vision of the episode. When you're on a show working for a showrunner, there are several points to consider: It is their show, their vision, and their voice that gives the final word on the script drafts presented to the studio, network, and production. While I had a logical understanding of this process, the practical application of it left me completely shocked to discover only about 25% of what we originally wrote was included in the studio draft of our script. It was the first time I'd written a script, and to only recognize a few of the words that I wrote was shocking; but in hindsight, it was also normal and to be expected.

It was a hard pill to swallow for me, but it was also a learning lesson that as staff writers, we're turning in scripts that will be transformed based on the vision of the people in charge. At that moment I realized, this is *not* my show. I loved writing on the show. I loved contributing to the show. It was a fun, exciting, iconic show to be a part of, but at the end of the day... it was not *my* show.

That's when I knew I wanted to have my own show. I'd thought about having my own show years prior when I first started working for Yvette. It took so long for me to become a writer that I was just so happy and grateful to finally be in a writers' room. I lost sight of one of my original dreams.

At that moment, I was reminded that I still had the desire to create and run something of my own and see it through from what initially is in my head, to what is actually presented to the audience. That's when both JaSheika and I shifted from *"impossible"* to *"I'm possible."* It was the first spark of conviction I had that one day we are going to run our own show.

JaSheika

As much as I loved working on *Empire,* it was at that time that I, too, realized we'd been playing small. We are creators ourselves. When we first dreamt of working in television, it was out of a desire to create and run our own show. But because the journey of getting into a writers' room and on staff was long and hard, we had tried to reconcile ourselves with the idea of being okay with being on staff, as long as we remained working consistently. We tried... and failed.

We hadn't come this far and worked this hard to just work for other people. After working consistently on various hit shows such as *Desperate Housewives, Dexter, Revenge,* and now *Empire,* I was reminded we weren't meant to only be writers on other people's shows just to stay employed. We were meant for more. As a writer on staff, your job is to support the showrunner's vision. While we've always been happy to do that, we've also had our own ideas and vision for shows. And to see our vision and ideas come to light, we would have to work hard to create our own show and push for our voices to be heard.

That's when our dreams fully shifted to being showrunners. We'd been so resistant to the idea of becoming people who run shows, but we couldn't resist it anymore. We've been gifted with the experiences we've had—working at studios and networks, on the productions of hit series, and working for badass female showrunners—and the knowledge we've gained from those combined experiences is invaluable. It would be crazy for us not to utilize our strengths in ways that fall in line with this new dream we desire.

We hadn't come this far and worked this hard to just work for other people.

JaNeika

Yvette has shared the moment she realized she had to create her own show. It was when she was on a TV show called *Hangin' with Mr. Cooper.* As the only Black female on the writing staff during the first season, she thought, *"If this is what working in TV is going to be like for the rest of my career, pretty soon I won't have one."* It was a light bulb moment for her. Although circumstances were very different for us on *Empire,* we also had a moment where light was shed on a realization: It's not impossible for us to create and run our own show. In fact, it is very possible. We just needed that kick of motivation—or spark of inspiration, however you choose to see it—to make it clear to us what we were capable of doing.

When JaSheika and I create our own shows, we want disadvantaged, at-risk youth who aspire to work in TV and film to have opportunities to visit and work on our sets, similar to the access and opportunity we had when we took our spring break trip to visit the set of *Dawson's Creek.* It was so important for the seed of possibility to be planted in us when we saw what it was like to be on the set of a TV series. We hope to one day create that same opportunity for others.

When I first started working as an intern for Yvette, I attended a gathering at her house and was surprised to encounter so many people she had worked with that I grew up watching on TV, including Kadeem Hardison and Darryl Bell, who played Dwayne Wayne and Ron Johnson on *A Different World.* I thought to myself, *"Oh my God. I used to watch you guys as a kid growing up in Germany."* It was truly surreal that this was my life—working with and being surrounded by creatives and artists I admired most of my life. Sitting in a living room with them, enjoying fresh food with plenty of laughs, I came to realize they were normal people… just like me. Having these, and several other full-circle moments, allowed me to see that when you close the gap between how you view yourself and the people who inspire you, possibilities begin to pour in. What initially may seem impossible can quickly evolve, shift, and become: *I'm possible.*

Chapter Seventeen

THE FUN IN FEAR

"From now on, we won't just face our worst fears, we will seek them out."

— Buffy, *Buffy the Vampire Slayer*

JaNeika

Seeing "fun in fear" is a completely different mindset we've taken on now, as compared to the one we had at the start of our careers. Because of various trials we've faced—the valleys amongst the peaks, like losing jobs, being unemployed for months at a time, questioning our purpose—instead of letting fear hinder our forward movement, we now say, *"Okay I'm scared, but how can I create joy in this moment, despite the fear?"*

Fear never goes away, no matter how successful one becomes. Take Beyoncé for example. When people watch her perform, they see a woman who takes to the stage and commands it with effort and grace. But even Beyoncé admittedly shared that she's nervous before every performance: *"If I'm nervous, I know I'm going to have a good show."*

For JaSheika and I, it doesn't matter what we achieve or how many great episodes of television we write, we still have to go back to a blank page whenever we start a new project, and that remains one of the scariest things ever. It's scary because of the underlying belief we won't be able to top our most recent completed work.

Years prior, we would have let fear cripple us in the writers' room. We were so fearful of disagreeing and dissenting with folks in the room, and the world in general. Now, instead of letting fear cripple us and prevent us from stating our opinions, we treat fear as a superpower. Fear informs when there is something we need to release. If there is a word, a feeling, a thought, or opinion we fight against saying out of fear of how it will be received, we pause now—and instead, respect that word, that feeling, that thought, or that opinion, by letting it out.

We're still growing and developing as writers and as TV show creators. Although we're currently one for one in selling a pilot, like most people, my voice still shakes when I speak publicly before any perceived VIPs (very important people). Pitching is performance—an art form that requires you to be at the center of a buyer's attention. Being at the center of anyone's attention is still very difficult for my sister and me. We're behind the cameras as writers for a reason. Today, instead of wallowing in how much we hate public speaking and being the center of attention, we have found new ways to embrace the joy and have fun with it.

JaSheika

As adults—particularly those who work in a very difficult industry—it's nice to have somebody who knows me inside and out, who completely understands my sensibility as a partner in the room, whether it's on set, in a network or studio office, or a writers' room. Whenever I stumble or am not clear on my thoughts, JaNeika always has my back when I need to argue a point that isn't comprehended or received well by others. We have a signal that we use extensively when tag-teaming a pitch, a story, or why we are strongly in support of a specific story direction. This has worked for us for years.

JaNeika

When it came time to pitch our first show—a drug queenpin drama called *Philly Reign*—our tag-teaming skills were tested when our first meeting was rescheduled during JaSheika's travels to Albania for her brother-in-law's wedding. As a result, I had to pitch it by myself for the first round of meetings. My sister's been my partner since we were in the womb together, so not having her with me for something so monumental—our first pitch—was frightening. It was also nerve-racking because we had rehearsed it so much, together; when she'd come in, when I'd make certain jokes. I wasn't so sure I could pull it off without her driving me.

When I went in to pitch to the first potential buyer and read the first part by myself, I was so used to having her read it with me, that my mouth dried up in the middle of speaking. I talked so much I had to stop and get water. I was ridiculously nervous and thought, *"Ugh, my voice sounds awful."* Afterward, I just kept thinking to myself, *"Well, this is horrible, but it's cool, it's just a practice run. It'll be fine."*

Although I was afraid throughout the first round, I pushed past the fear and did it anyway. I casually engaged with all the executives in each room I pitched, and when JaSheika returned, we were back in lockstep like she had never left. Out of the more than ten networks and platforms we pitched to that were interested in the show, we ultimately went with USA Network.

Mary J. Blige will be the executive producer of the series, based on the real-life story of Thelma Wright. Thelma, a woman married to a big-time drug dealer in Philadelphia in the '80s, was devastated upon discovering her husband was murdered by one of his distributors. Unbeknownst to her family, friends, cops, and her husband's competitors, she ended up taking over his business. As a result, she became known as the queen of Philly.

Developing Ms. Thelma's story has brought us incredible joy, and we are so excited to be a part of the team that is bringing it to life. We are in the process of writing and developing the pilot script that we hope will be picked up to shoot and greenlit to series in the coming months.

Creating joy around fear is such an incredible way to tackle it. Fear is always going to be around us, so why not put faith over fear, and instead have fun with it? That little seed to become showrunners, initially planted five years ago, is another example of something we have spoken into existence. This time, however, it took less than ten years to actualize the dream.

Chapter Eighteen

FRANKLY, MY DEAR, I DON'T GIVE A DAMN: USING OUR AUTHENTIC VOICE

"In what universe, for one second, would you think I was threatened by you?"

— Amanda Woodward, *Melrose Place*

JaSheika

When I was in high school, I had a really good friend named Terrance Solomon and I remember him asking me, *"Why do you care about what other people think?"* The fact that I shouldn't care always stuck with me in my head but applying it in practice took me a long time.

For so long, I was concerned about saying the right things and being perfect. When I was in a relationship in high school, I got into an argument with my boyfriend at the time, and instead of having a conversation in person, I wrote a letter and pulled it out to read to him because I wanted to make sure I didn't forget anything. I poured my heart out to him and when I finished, he started laughing because he thought it was so ridiculous that I couldn't just come out and say what I needed to say. I needed to write it down on paper.

I'm still self-conscious when I try to express myself when pitching. I have thoughts in my head, but I'm not always quick to share them. I need time to think, to sit in a room alone and process my thoughts first. When I was working on my first show as a writer, I would see people pitch ideas and I would get so excited about them. I would write my ideas down on paper, like a warming-up process before a performance. I wanted to be thoughtful about what I said because if I didn't say it properly, I thought it wouldn't land—people would get offended or misinterpret what I had to say. So, I didn't say much. I think that had a lot to do with why the showrunner who didn't pick up my option was so disappointed in me. He said, *"I'd see you write things on paper and I was waiting but you never delivered."*

I never wanted anybody to have anything to hold against me. I knew how much I judged myself, so I was sure others would judge me even harsher. As I've gotten older and more seasoned, I have let that fear go. I've developed a "not giving a shit complex." I don't care so much about what people think because I realize that it doesn't matter what I do or don't say, people are going to judge me regardless. Once I came to that realization, I was able to release my anxiety and reluctance, and pitch without shame.

Again, as Mark Perry, told me: *"Pitch without shame. Nobody's perfect."* As creatives, we have to let fear of judgment go because we're not going to please everybody with what we create. The true expression of ourselves is what is most important.

JaNeika is much better at shamelessly pitching than I am; she'll say the most outlandish things, relay outrageous thoughts, or give her honest opinion about various subjects fearlessly, regardless of what other people think. At times, people are like, *"OMG!"* or *"What?"* But they respect her for being honest and speaking her mind freely, and often they wish they were so bold. The benefit of pitching without shame is that freedom builds confidence and strength in your voice.

Fear is always going to be around us, so why not put faith over fear, and instead have fun with it?

JaNeika

I take it back to watching shows when I was a kid with our grandmother, Ma. There's this character on *All My Children*, Erica Kane's long-lost daughter, named Kendall. I hated Kendall when I was growing up, but when I got older, I respected the character because she says and does what I wished I could but didn't have the guts to do. I cared too much about what people were going to say or how they would feel about me.

The character of Cookie in *Empire* is similar. She says things that may not necessarily be politically correct or popular, but people can relate to her because they have these thoughts and opinions, too. They just are not brave enough to say them out loud. I feel that's how everyone should be in real life—say what's on your mind, not rudely or disrespectfully, but in a way that is true to yourself.

I've come to the point where it's difficult for me to respect people if they aren't revealing their authentic self. We work in television with other creatives who are sensitive and can, therefore, receive some of the things we say in ways they are not intended. When I first got staffed, it was a little daunting how people tip-toed around giving their opinions because they were operating from a fear of offending others, instead of being truthful. Polite isn't necessarily authentic.

JaSheika

One of the factors that makes a hit show is a room full of writers who don't always agree with each other. Something JaNeika and I have learned while working in writers' rooms is that sometimes we can be so cognizant of not offending others, that we instead offend ourselves by not being true to who we are. We should be able to operate in every area of our lives, but particularly in our professional lives, being true to our authentic selves.

Chapter Nineteen

I AM... THE POWER OF DECLARATION AND DREAMING BIGGER

"Your wish is my command."

— Jeannie, *I Dream of Jeannie*

JaSheika

JaNeika and I have affirmations that we recently put into practice whenever we are in doubt, have concerns, or just want to feel good. They are manifestation mantras we say to ourselves that remind us and reaffirm who we are and what we are capable of.

When we were in London, we went on a trip to Harry Potter World at Leavesden Studios, where they shot all of the *Harry Potter* films. It felt as if we were walking into a theme park as we stood in the enormous line, waiting to get inside for the tour. People of all ages, cultures, and backgrounds gathered amongst us, filled with excitement as we all finally entered to embark upon our tour of the stages (the fantastical world of Hogwarts).

There was no shame in the fact that we were grown women; but the sheer pleasure, joy, and glee I felt in that moment was a dream come true—similar to the feeling we had years before when we visited the set of *Dawson's Creek*. We entered the chambers of Hogwarts and the closet where Harry was forced to room in his childhood home. We got to see and take pictures of the original costumes, got a firsthand glimpse of the secrets behind some of the greatest visual effects, and got insight into the makings and magic of this epic book series that extended into eight motion pictures.

Seeing what was created out of J.K. Rowling's mind and vision was incredibly magical. We went on the tour and they started talking about how many people were employed there over the years as a result of her imagination. It was soul-affirming to see firsthand the intricate details it took to bring the series to life for years, and to hear how loyal and committed the crewmembers were. For decades, they poured their hearts and souls into their craft, all in an effort to ensure that what we saw onscreen was a reflection of their utmost dedication, love, and respect for J.K. and the world she envisioned on the page.

I looked up and I prayed, *"God, I want to create a world where I can employ people for ten years and beyond like J.K. Rowling, and have audiences all over the globe clamoring for the next installment of my work as a writer. I want to leave a legacy."*

I went home and wrote out a contract: *"I am a powerful, risk-taking, authentic leader, creating abundance for myself and others."* That statement summarized what I want to do and apply to all aspects of my life. Even today, I'll either say that mantra or repeat affirmations like, *"I'm successful, I'm focused."* Whatever it is that I want to be, I am.

JaNeika

I ground myself daily through affirmation, repeating to myself: *"I am a trusting, powerful, and giving leader."* I recently took a solo trip to Mexico to prioritize wellness and self-care. While I was there, enjoying the sun, the beach, and the all-inclusive relaxation in solitude, I encountered a healer at the spa I visited, daily, throughout my vacation. After completing a traditional, ritual massage treatment, the healer came out and said to me: *"You are a goddess who is full of love."* Those were some powerful words that took a moment for me to receive. After a while, I thought... *Why not?* This was a statement for me to take ownership of because, through declaration, I have the power to create who I want to be. Whenever I say, *"I am"* and call in what I need, what I need is given to me. So, I am a goddess who is full of love, ready to take on the world and all of the endless possibilities it has in store for me. There is true power in declaring your "I AM."

JaSheika

We were speaking to seventh and eighth graders at a camp once when we said, *"Whatever it is that you want, just say it—call it out to the universe because you don't know how it's going to happen."* I truly believe in the power of your words. Calling your dreams out loud is like planting a seed into the universe that will eventually grow and catch up to you. I'm always impressed with how kids hear what we have to say. Almost immediately after sharing this belief with them, they declared, *"I'm going to be a singer!"* or *"I'm going to be a basketball star!"* They were putting their dreams out there and spoke them into the future with ease.

There's a lot of power in declaring. JaNeika and I declared where we wanted to be within ten years. We declared getting onto a number of shows we worked on. We declared getting the jobs that we wanted. We declared that we would one day become showrunners and executive producers of our own shows. As we continue the practice of declaration, we continue to bring out the worlds that are deep within our wildest dreams into our reality.

Empire ended its series run after six seasons. We ended our run on the show as supervising producers and began working on a new Netflix series as co-executive producers. As JaNeika mentioned, we're

We are always dreaming bigger because there are no limits to how many dreams we can have.

also developing a pilot at USA we're executive producing, along with Mary J. Blige, titled *Philly Reign*. Our dreams won't stop there, however.

We're always dreaming bigger because there are no limits to how many dreams we can have. After we accomplish one dream, we move into another, because our dreams are constant and continue to grow. We are "living double" proof that dreams are forever evolving, and in due time, will inevitably come true.

Conclusion:

SWEET DREAMS OR A BEAUTIFUL NIGHTMARE: THE GOOD, THE BAD, AND THE TRUE TEA ABOUT ACHIEVING YOUR DREAMS

We hope you've enjoyed this book, but before we round out this particular writing journey, we want to take a moment and reiterate a few points about dream-chasing, dream-achieving, and life after the dream. Often when we share our journeys of success, a few blind spots are left unseen. To make sure that is not the case here, we want to touch on a few points that we hope you can take with you on the road to fulfilling your dreams.

It is truly a blessed experience being able to follow your dreams and watch them come to life because of the faith, work, support, and effort you've put into them. Just like the five points of story that take us through the journey of a television episode, as well as our lives, here are five key points we hope you can take away from our story and keep in mind as the journey toward your wildest dreams continues.

With gratitude and belief in the power of your dreams,

JaNeika and *JaSheika*

1. DON'T STOP DREAMING

As mentioned in the last chapter, once the dream has arrived, it doesn't mean you've arrived at your final destination. What we're not often told about reaching our dreams and completing our biggest goals is that once we do, the grass doesn't become greener, and the world is not suddenly perfect.

Dream achievement means you've worked your butt off to receive something in your life that took a period of hard work and dedication. But, more hard work, obstacles to overcome, and difficult times are still things we face, sometimes even more so after the dream is fulfilled. The good news is, the journey to get where you are has prepared you to face all of it.

Once you've hit your goal, great! There's more dreaming to be had because dream achievement is proof positive that even more dreams have yet to be fulfilled. *"So, what's next?"* you should ask yourself. Just like the business is ever-evolving, your interests and dreams will also continue to evolve. You're not limited to just one dream come true per lifetime, or three—this isn't *Aladdin*, and there are no genies around.

2. STAND OUT ABOVE THE CROWD... WITH INTEGRITY AND ACCOUNTABILITY

We're going to let you in on a secret. There are two simple characteristics you should have in order to stand out and get a head start on fulfilling your dreams: Have **integrity** and be **accountable** for your actions.

The reality is, as professionals, we have not always been in integrity. There are deadlines we have missed, mistakes we have made... but when it comes to being accountable for our actions—good or bad—we always stand up. Don't get us wrong, it took us a while to get here, but we all start from somewhere, and now we're here.

When you fall out of integrity—which many of us do as imperfect humans—it's important to be accountable and acknowledge it. Although many of us tend to hold on to looking "good" or "perfect" in the eyes of our peers or bosses, what goes a long way in the minds of most in any profession is admitting when we are wrong. Acknowledge your faults, apologize, and move on. DO NOT lie or throw other people under the bus for your actions.

3. F.E.A.R: IT'S REAL AND HERE TO STAY

Fear of success is not a myth. It's a very real thing. We all experience it, even after we've successfully achieved our dreams. It comes up in various forms and stages in our lives; we can have a fear of actually realizing the dream we've spent so many years focused on, or a fear that if our dreams come to light, we somehow don't deserve it, or a fear that once we've achieved one dream, any others will never see the light of day.

The reality is, once we've achieved a dream, it's proof that we can successfully achieve so many more. What we cannot do is allow the fear of success—whether it's initial success or continued success—impede upon our achievements. All too often, we let the fear of arriving where we want to be prevent us from actually getting there. When it comes to discussing our journeys of achievement, we don't often speak about the fear in our heads that prevents us from moving forward. We could be right there, on the cusp of our breakthrough, but instead, choose to walk away because of fear.

Instead of being consumed and overwhelmed to the point of crippling inaction, we take a different approach to how we look at it. For us, fear is:

Fun and **E**xciting when **A**chievement Becomes **R**eality.

If you are facing fear while trying to achieve a dream, you can shift your perspective to joy for what's to come. You are creating what's next and that's what you should allow yourself to be excited about—the fact that you get to bring to the world that which it has yet to see.

4. THE PRIVILEGE OF BEING UNDERESTIMATED

As women... women of color... Black women who work in a male-dominated industry, we're often underestimated. As "successful" as we're considered today, when we walk into meetings and public spaces, we're still constantly underestimated. It's an experience we've reconciled ourselves with, and for the most part, have come to expect.

Being underestimated as women in any forum is very real and ever-present, but if we focus on the problems that come with being underestimated time and time again, we miss the opportunities that come along with that underestimation. The truth is, being underestimated equates to the bar being set so low for us to achieve, we consistently smack it down each time we overachieve, as we're naturally inclined to do. When people underestimate what you're capable of, let them. Their own limited beliefs will have them mesmerized by the magic of your natural talent and accomplishment. It is not your job to disprove their beliefs—eventually, they'll learn.

Allowing someone else to project her hang-ups and iniquities onto us as dreamers takes away from our creativity. Who has time for that? Not us! Instead of letting a circumstance like someone else's low expectations and non-belief in your possibility prevent you from achievement, you have a choice: channel that energy and use it as motivation to prove your doubters wrong... or ignore them altogether and simply focus on your work. The choice is yours, but as you continue to rise in your career, it will quickly become clear—all along, you've never had anything to prove. You just simply have to *be*.

5. SEE IT TO BELIEVE IT

Lastly, to see the dream, you must be the dream—before it even happens. Envision where you want to be and how you want to feel when it comes to the things that you want. See it! It is a crucial part of making your dreams come true. It's also why dream scaping and vision boarding are extremely useful when it comes to actualizing your dreams.

All too often we hold ourselves so far away from the goals we want, as if they're too good to be true in our own lives. It's those beliefs that keep us from seeing the possibilities that lead to our dreams becoming our reality. Sometimes it's our own mindsets—or lack of imagining ourselves exactly where we want to be— that serve as the primary obstacles to our dreams coming true.

BONUS: IN A COMPETITION OF ONE AND ONE ONLY!

Here's a little something extra for you guys. A reminder: the only person you are competing with is YOU. All too often, we either pit ourselves against others, or others pit us against our peers out of a false sense of motivation. The belief that competition breeds better work is one that comes out of both fear and scarcity.

Real talk? When we think of ourselves as being in competition with someone, nine times out of ten, we've never even crossed that person's radar. It's false motivation to embrace a narrative of being in competition with others. The reality is there is no reason to compare and contrast ourselves to other people, observing them as obstacles to our success, when we can instead enlist them as allies.

The benefit of competing with yourself is that you're constantly pushing yourself to grow above your last greatest accomplishment. Being in a competition of one means there is room for more wins. The idea that in order for you to win, someone else has to lose is an unproven fact—simply put, it's BS. Here is an alternative idea to ponder: There is *always* room for more wins. Try embracing the idea of "win-win." Instead of racing against the competition, race against yourself and see how you can bring your peers along with you for the ride.

A Few of Our Favorite TV Shows That Inspired Us Growing Up...

227

90210

A Different World

Alf

Alias

All My Children

Ally McBeal

Another World

Beauty and the Beast

Benson

Bewitched

Buffy the Vampire Slayer

California Dreams

Cheers

Coach

Dallas

Dark Shadows

Dark Wing Duck

Dawson's Creek

Days of Our Lives

Designing Women

Desperate Housewives

Different Strokes

Dobie Gillis

Doogie Howser, M.D.

Duck Tales

Dynasty

Empty Nest

Falcon Crest

Family Matters

Family Ties

Felicity

Fifteen

Fraggle Rock

Full House

Gargoyles

General Hospital

Gilligan's Island

Gimme a Break!

Good Times

Goof Troop

Green Acres

Gummy Bears

Hang Time

Hangin' with Mr. Cooper

Happy Days

Heathcliff

Hercules

Hotel

I Dream of Jeannie

In Living Color

In the Heat of the Night

Jake and the Fat Man

Kim Possible

Knots Landing

Laverne & Shirley

Living Single

Lizzie McGuire

MacGyver

Magnum, P.I.

Married with Children

Martin

Melrose Place

Mighty Morphin Power Rangers

Models Inc.

Moesha

Moonlighting

Mork and Mindy

Mr. Belvedere

Mr. Ed

Mr. Rogers' Neighborhood

Murder She Wrote

My Brother and Me

My Little Pony

Night Court

Ocean Girl

One Life to Live

Out of This World

Patty Duke

Perfect Strangers

Perry Mason

Punky Brewster

Rainbow Bright

Reading Rainbow

Ready or Not

Sabrina the Teenage Witch

Saved by the Bell

Scandal

Sesame Street

Sister Kate

Sister, Sister

Small Wonder

Star Trek

Star Trek: The Next Generation

Step by Step

Strawberry Shortcake

Tail Spin

Teenage Mutant Ninja Turtles

That's So Raven

The Andy Griffith Show

The Care Bears

The Cosby Show

The Flintstones

The Golden Girls

The Good Wife

The Jetsons

The Love Boat

The Muppets

The Nanny

The Proud Family

The Secret World of Alex Mac

The Simpsons

The Smurfs

The Wonder Years

The Wuzzles

The Young and The Restless

Three's Company

What's Happening, Now?

What's Happening?

Who's the Boss

X-Men

Xena Warrior Princess

ACKNOWLEDGMENTS

We are blessed. Abundantly blessed beyond measure because of God and the people placed in our lives to help guide us on our journey and path to success in Hollywood. But the truth is, success has come in many different phases and stages of our lives.

We are so grateful to our parents, Eugene 'Geno' James and Angela Likely, for instilling in us that our dreams are inevitable possibilities, and for gifting us with the creative minds that enabled us to pursue them. Our grandmother, Annie Ruth Rhodes, for helping to raise us, and introducing us to Victor Newman and Erica Kane. Our grandfather, Clifford Stallworth, for bringing God to the forefront of our lives. Our Auntie Pat for showing us what it means to be disciplined and hardworking, and our Uncle Tyrone for introducing us to regimen. Our stepmother, Felecia James, for showing us what it truly means to love purely and unconditionally. Our cousins, Jerrell & Jacqueline Sheppard, Stephanie Stallworth, Jamesa Stallworth, and brother, Marcus Jones, for challenging us and supporting us through everything we do. The village of family and friends who have been with us since we were babies, praying for us, supporting us, and inspiring us. (Cynthia Williams, Uncle Junior and Kattie, Uncle Ricky, Auntie Marion, Shon & Shan, Grandma Ethel, Auntie Desta and Uncle Lewis, Kienon & Tori Lewis, Uncle Raymond, Gary Likely, The Finkleys and The Stallworths, Sharon Hines, Annette Williams, Sam and Rhonda Ferguson, Sametris Ferguson, Natarsha Williams, Carinah Tané McKinnie, Lisa DeBlanc), Auntie Diane and the entire James family.

To my husband, Francesko Bushi, for reminding us about our ability to shift our perspective and soar. And to my loving and supportive in-laws, the Bushi family.

To all of our friends, we want to thank you for your unconditional love and support throughout this journey. You've never once left our side, and because of you we are blessed beyond measure. (Alecia "Neenee" Fields, Jennifer Reece Boatwright, Sue Carrion, Brandy Brown, Sabina Frederick, Mioshi Hill, LaTonya

Croff, Justin Grant, Terrence Solomon, Nancy Cruz, Sandra Quinonés, Courtney Brown, Heather Alexander, Reyna Gilmore, Mohammed Abukhdeir, Julio Calderon, Joseph Perdomo, Bennie Greene Jr., Andrea Guerrier, Tiffany Burt, Binta Moncur, Suezette Robotham, James Andrews, Marlon Furlongue, Mrs. Marva Furlongue, Angela Quijano, Angie Davis, Karla King, Kwanzaa Brown, Evelyn Harris, Cruz Bueno Meta, Julio Bueno, Natalie Domond, Jessica Jones, April Qualls, Fallon & Felisha King, Bernard Harvey, Firas Quick, Seema Thakker, Tara Varilek, Jordan Marinov, Kristen Carter, Jamila Jordan, Mrs. Donna Jordan, Mrs. Pamela Marshall, Katie Kyme, Kristen Saberre, Jennifer Gomez, Vero Gomez, Kerri Berney, Rachel Spenst, Khadija Brockington, Dorian Chandler, Nicole Thomas, Nicole Jones, Yvette Foy, Crystal Jenkins, Yvette Carter, Lorena Mora, Tameka Nelson, Tiffany Nelson-Hobbs, Raney Branch, Nikki Marshall, Josh Pineda, Carlos Ramos, Carlton Hickman, Sonia Evans, Jess Pineda, Olivia Reyes, Katie Gruel, Sabrina Warda, Zac Hill, Nathan Cheney, Tony Towns, Stephen Serulla, Paul Cordova, Holly Brown, Tracey Brown, Karie Gonia, Golebahar Tabatabai, Joe Fazzio, Chuck Hayward, Aaron Carew, David McMillan, Jill Uyeda, Kevin Scott, David Robinson Jr., Temple Northup, Carla Waddles, CECI, Elizabeth Insalaco, Mary Ruiz, Minnette & Gino Garcia, Mr. Bill & Mary Jane Woodward, Mrs. Thelma Wright, Jacky Wright, our LA Writers' Group, our Momentum Education Family, and the lovely women of our prayer and Bible study groups).

To our teachers, bosses, and mentors, your light has guided and propelled us to this moment. Because of you we continue reaching higher. (Yvette Lee Bowser, Jean Hester, Victoria LaFortune, Celia Hamel, Dawn Soler, Channing Dungey, Angela Nissel, Nne Ebong, Mike Kelley, Wendy Calhoun, Charles Murray, Maggie Malina, Sharon Horgan, Jen Crittenden, Gaby Allan, Dr. James Babanikos, Dr. Julian Williams, Fiona Chew, Richard Dubin, Michael Schoonmaker, Shelly Griffin, Andrea Asimow, Jennifer Williams, David Wyatt, Michael Ajakwe Jr., Gina Reyes)

To all of our colleagues, past and present, in particular, the Creators and Producers of *Empire*, Writers, Cast, and the entire Crew, and especially Attica Locke, Trai Byers, Grace Byers, Gabourey Sidibe, Tasha Smith, and Jussie Smollett: Thank you for inspiring us, pushing us, and loving us as we continue to dream.

To our amazing team: Howie Tanenbaum, Michael Botti, Lauren Partipillo-Schwartz, and Duncan Hedges; thank you for always rooting and going hard for us, every step of the way.

Our awesome glam team: Ursula Campbell, Lari Maxx, Walid Azami, Jordana David, Andrew Nguyen, thank you for not only enhancing what is within, but for nurturing our minds and spirits. All of you make us feel good in ways we've never experienced until now. Thank you!

And a very special thank you to Carolynn Smith-Jones and Kristen Rumberger, of Seven Marketing PR and PWR Press Publishing, for your undeniable patience, and for always believing in, and urging us to share, our story. Thank you, Karen and Allison for getting us started.

If we missed anyone please know that it was not purposeful and do NOT think for one second that we've dismissed the impact you have had on our lives. We love and appreciate all of you. Charge it to our heads and not our hearts.

ABOUT THE AUTHORS

JaNeika and JaSheika James have had an ongoing love affair with film and television since childhood. It wasn't until college that the twin sisters decided to pursue careers in film and TV, both graduating with bachelor's degrees in Telecommunication from the University of Florida's College of Journalism. While sharing common goals to write for television, JaNeika and JaSheika have taken very different paths in achieving those goals.

Upon graduating from the University of Florida, JaSheika went on to work for the hit series, *DESPERATE HOUSEWIVES* and *DEXTER,* and later in post-production at ABC Studios. Her professional experience in the writers' room began on ABC's *REVENGE,* where she joined the writing staff in the third season.

Following JaNeika's master's studies at Syracuse University's Newhouse School of Public Communication, she had the opportunity to interview Yvette Lee Bowser, Creator and Executive Producer of the hit FOX television series *LIVING SINGLE.* She began her career working for Mrs. Bowser on UPN's *HALF & HALF.* JaNeika went on to work under the producing team of Jennifer Crittenden and Gabrielle Allan (*SEINFELD, SCRUBS, WHAT'S YOUR NUMBER?*) at ABC Studios, and later in Scripted Development at VH1.

JaNeika and JaSheika rose up the ranks from Staff Writers to Supervising Producers on Fox's groundbreaking hit series, *EMPIRE.* Currently, they serve as Co-Executive Producers on HBO Max's *GOSSIP GIRL,* and are developing a USA pilot, *PHILLY REIGN,* as executive producers alongside Oscar-Nominated actress, Mary J. Blige. They are committed to creating, developing, and writing projects that enlighten, inspire, and entertain audiences around the world.

Made in the USA
Middletown, DE
02 March 2021

34633031R00106